THE ARTFUL DODGER'S GUIDE TO

PLANNING YOUR ESTATE

Fifth Edition

Thomas Hart Hawley

Cover Illustrated by Shell Fisher

Adams Media
Avon, Massachusetts

Original Cover Design: Irene Imfeld Graphic Design
Copy Editor: Diane H. Gibbs
Advisor: Jack Howell

The fourth edition was published by Linthicum Press, Carmel-by-the-Sea, CA.

Published by Adams Media, an F+W Publications Company
57 Littlefield Street, Avon, MA 02322
www.adamsmedia.com

ISBN: 1-58062-949-0

J I H G F E D C B A

Printed in United States of America.

Library of Congress Cataloging-in-Publication Data
Hawley, Thomas Hart.
The artful dodger's guide to planning your estate /
Thomas Hart Hawley.—5th ed.
p.   cm.
ISBN 1-58062-949-0
1. Finance, Personal. 2. Estate planning. I. Title.
HG179.H3443 2004
332.024'01—dc21
2003012549

This publication is intended to provide accurate information about selected estate planning
topics. It is not meant to be a substitute for working directly with a qualified attorney or
other estate planning professional, but rather is meant to help the reader prepare for such
work. This book is sold with the understanding that the author and the publisher are not
engaged in rendering to the reader any legal, accounting, tax, or other professional services.
Every attempt has been made to ensure the accuracy of the material here presented, but neither the author nor the publisher assumes liability for any error or omission.

Many of the designations used by manufacturers and sellers to distinguish their products are
claimed as trademarks. Where those designations appear in this book and Adams Media was
aware of a trademark claim, the designations have been printed with initial capital letters.

This book is available at quantity discounts for bulk purchases.
For information, call 1-800-872-5627.

This book is dedicated to my parents,
to my own little Dodgers,
Inga and Kristina,
and to the memory of John Kaplan,
Professor of Law, Stanford University.

CONTENTS

Conclusion

Appendices

AUTHOR'S FOREWORD TO FIFTH EDITION

The first edition of this book sold well. This may be more a reflection of the size of my family than the merits of the book. Nonetheless, encouraged, I set about working on the second edition.

Roughly ten minutes after the second edition had been printed, Uncle Sam announced the passage of the 1998 Tax Relief Act. The second edition was out of date before its ink had dried.

Undaunted, I set about writing the third edition, which I changed to a national edition. Of course, I updated the edition to include the 1998 Tax Relief Act.

The fourth edition was further updated to include the new IRA regulations that came out in January of 2001 and information about state tuition programs as well. It came off the presses in April of 2001. In June Uncle Sam gave us the 2001 Tax Relief Act at which point the price of the fourth edition immediately became negotiable. Updating this book was becoming a mug's game.

This fifth edition, updated with the 2001 Tax Relief Act, also includes information on Pooled Income funds—a great charitable device for those readers too cheap to hire a Clever Attorney.

The 2001 Tax Relief Act has complicated estate planning in general and the writing of this book in particular. One might well ask, why should I spend money to plan my estate, or for that matter, to buy your book if estate taxes are going to disappear after 2009? The problem is that under current law estate taxes return, after a one-year repeal, in 2011. And, perhaps more important, most observers believe that, in view of the threat of terrorism, our involvement in foreign wars, and soaring deficits, Uncle Sam will be forced to rethink the repeal of death taxes. So we are truly in limbo and have little choice but continue to implement strategies calculated to reduce or eliminate estate taxes (if any).

I can only hope that the next major tax act, when it comes along, will be far enough in the future to give this edition a chance.

ACKNOWLEDGMENTS

I want to thank the following for their criticism (constant but, usually, constructive) of the first draft of this book: Jim Cook, Esq., Sandra Farrell, Marijke Hartog, Charles Hawley, Kate Hawley, Melvin Hawley, Esq., Richard Henson, Esq., Michael L. McMahan, Esq., and W. R. Rosecrans, Esq.

I am especially grateful to Doug Thompson, editor of *The Carmel Pine Cone*, for agreeing to take a chance on the column "Where There's a Will . . .," and the many Carmel subscribers (well, actually two) who urged me to write this book.

Thanks also to the long-suffering efforts of my paralegal of twenty-six years, Carol Jarick, for her technical assistance and advice.

And to my running buddy, Shell Fisher, whose brilliant illustrations breathe life into the characters in this book.

I did my own word processing for this book. Every few minutes or so my computer screen would flash some message like "Error message number 23 reading floppy disk drive: 1. Retry 2. Cancel 3. Commit seppuku." Thank goodness for my friend and computer guru, Howard Nieman, who never complained about the late-night calls and always had a solution.

I wish to express my gratitude to Harold Boucher for his practical suggestions and the inspiration of his excellent book, *California Living Trusts and Wills* (Pennoyer Press, 1994).

Additionally, I wish to acknowledge the truly scrutinous efforts of the copy editors, Diane H. Gibbs and Mark Woodworth, and the superb cover and text design by Irene Imfeld Graphic Design.

After this book was first published, a number of attorneys and other professionals provided very helpful comments on how it could be improved. My thanks to Yvonne A. Ascher, Esq., Elizabeth C. Gianola, Esq., Thomas E. Mallett, Esq., Sidney M. Morris, Esq., John Northcote,

Esq., Jo Marie Ometer, Esq., William S. Soskin, James E. Stiles, C.P.A., Mark J. Welch, Esq., and Klar Wennerholm, Esq.

The most difficult chapters for me to write were the three on retirement planning (Chapters 26–27). It took the efforts of Ute Isbill, Esq., and my law partner, Kathleen Llewellyn, Esq., who provided the initial outline, to get me started, and the professional assistance of Michael J. Jones, C.P.A., the dean of retirement planners, who put the finishing touches on the chapters.

And finally, this book would not have happened without the unflagging efforts of Jack Howell of Morning Sun Press, who shepherded the project from first draft to final publication.

INTRODUCTION

Allow me to introduce The Artful Dodger. "Art," as he is known to his friends, is undergoing a midlife crisis. At Art's age this would not be unusual except that Art's crisis is different. While most men his age suddenly go out and spend gobs of money on a red Boxster convertible, Art suddenly wants to save gobs of money, through estate planning.

He is aided by his "Clever Attorney," who not only gives Art sound advice but also, on occasion, keeps him from doing something really stupid.

In these pages you will also meet Ellie Dodger, Art's wife, along with the Dodgers' son, Roger, and Roger's kids, the six little Dodgers, along with sundry other Dodger relations.

The villain of the piece, of course, is Uncle Sam, who doggedly tries to deprive Art of his hard-earned booty.

The Dodgers will help illustrate the ways all of us can save both income and estate taxes through basic planning techniques.

This is not a "do-it-yourself" book. Quite the contrary. Estate planning is complex and best left to the experts. Instead, this book will give you the basics you need to better assist your own Clever Attorney in planning your estate. By knowing something about estate planning before consulting your attorney, you will save yourself both time and money.

Nor is this book about exotic tax loopholes that are fabulous if they work and disastrous if they don't. The techniques discussed here are well established and, if implemented by a professional, will not come back to disturb your sleep.

Within these pages you will not learn how to avoid paying your fair share of taxes. Rather, you will learn how to minimize the impact of taxes on you and your family by making use of strategies to which Uncle Sam himself, albeit grudgingly, has consented.

Finally, this book is an overview. It is not intended to make a lawyer out of you. Every tax rule has an exception and every exception has a qualification and so on. These complexities may be fascinating to lawyers, but to most folks, they are a bore. To encourage you to read past page 16, I have left out a lot of the tedious stuff.

One word of caution: Uncle Sam is a regular Prince Hamlet when it comes to making up his mind. He is always fiddling with the tax law. So be on guard for changes he may make after this book is published.

Much of the material in this book first appeared in a weekly newspaper column called "Where There's a Will . . . ." For this reason, the chapters are column length, which is helpful in allowing you to traverse estate planning one short step at a time.

So come join Art and his family in what I hope will be a worthwhile and even entertaining journey to this foreign land of QTIPs, QDOTs, and QPRTs. And if you pay close attention, you might just save enough in taxes to have that red Boxster convertible.

NUTS AND BOLTS

The Artful Dodger has become obsessed lately with the idea of saving taxes. You can't blame Art. He comes by it honestly. For it was Art's grandfather Cornelius who, plagiarizing a famous philosopher, was fond of saying, "He who does not understand taxes is doomed to overpay them."

With the help of the Dodger clan, this little book explains in simple terms planning techniques that can save you and your family from the often devastating effect of death taxes. You cannot understand these techniques without knowing a little about our federal estate and gift tax system. Therefore, the first two chapters will provide you with an overview of this system.

To spare you a good deal of mind-numbing verbiage, what follows has been kept to a simple nuts-and-bolts description.

Estate and Gift Taxes
Uncle Sam taxes gifts you make during your life and at death. In medieval times (i.e., before 1977) lifetime gifts were taxed at a different rate from gifts made at death. Today the same tax rates apply to all gifts, whether they are made during life or at death.

The Estate Tax Exemption
The good news is that each of you has an estate tax exemption equal to $1,500,000 in 2004 and 2005, increasing to $2,000,000 in 2006, 2007, and 2008; and to $3,500,000 in 2009. In 2010 you have no exemption because there is no estate tax. But, unless Uncle Sam comes to the rescue, in 2011 the exemption returns to the exemption amount in

2001, which was $1,000,000. I know to a lot of you this tax scheme sounds totally nuts. This is because it is totally nuts. It is also totally unfair. In the case of two identically wealthy families, for example, the difference between a taxpayer who dies a few seconds on the near side of December 31, 2010, as opposed to one who dies a few seconds on the far side could be millions of dollars in estate taxes. (In this book, I will use $1,500,000 as the exemption amount, although you and I know it is a moving target.)

This exemption allows you to give away at your death $1,500,000 (or the current exemption amount) free of any estate tax. Let's assume, hypothetically that Grandfather Cornelius died leaving his $2,000,000 estate to his favorite grandson, Art Dodger. (Unfortunately, this is purely hypothetical since Grandfather C actually left all his loot to a twenty-six-year-old aromatherapist, but that's another story.) The first $1,500,000 would pass free of tax. Art would pay a whopping $225,000 on the remaining $500,000 because the bad news is that tax rates start out high.

The first dollar over $1,500,000 is taxed at 45%. Rates gradually increase until they reach 48% on estates exceeding $2,000,000. (Under the 2001 Tax Relief Act, starting in 2002, the top rate gradually declines to 45% by 2009.)

The Gift Tax Exemption

Some more good news is that each of you also has a gift tax exemption equal to $1,000,000, which allows you to give away during your life up to $1,000,000 free of any gift tax. Gift tax rates are the same as estate tax rates. Except, in 2010, when estate taxes go away, the highest gift tax rate will be 35%. But bear in mind that to the extent you use up your gift tax exemption during your life, your estate tax exemption is reduced at your death. So if Grandfather Cornelius had given Art $1,000,000 during his life, his estate tax exemption would be reduced from $1,500,000 to $500,000 at his death.

Annual Exclusion Gifts

Uncle Sam also allows you to give $11,000 each year to each of any number of people tax-free. (This used to be $10,000 but beginning in

1998 the amount of the annual exclusion adjusts upward for inflation in $1,000 increments.) Annual exclusion gifts do not reduce either your gift tax exemption or your estate tax exemption and therefore offer dramatic tax-saving opportunities. For example, Art has one child, Roger Dodger, and six grandchildren, the little Dodgers. Art can give $11,000 to each of these family members and instantly reduce his taxable estate by $77,000. In fact, if Art makes the gift on the evening of December 31, he can make another gift the next morning, as soon as his head has cleared, and remove a total of $154,000 from his estate in a matter of hours!

Uncle Sam used to disallow any gifts made within three years of death as presumably being made "in contemplation of death." But no more. Now even a deathbed gift works.

The Unlimited Marital Deduction

Since 1981, transfers between spouses during lifetime or at death are not taxed. The transfers must be outright (or in other qualifying forms, which we will get into later).

In theory, Art could leave his entire estate to his wife, Ellie Dodger (wake up, sports fans, that's a pun), who could then leave the estate to her new, presumably younger, husband, who could later leave the estate to his new, presumably younger, wife, and so on. In this way, theoretically, fortunes could pass down through the ages untaxed. In reality, most of us cannot get too excited about estate plans calculated to save taxes for our posthumous marital replacements.

Now let's take a look at how death taxes are computed. Then we will roll up our sleeves and begin looking at various ways of avoiding these taxes.

MORE NUTS AND BOLTS

*L*et's see just how Uncle Sam goes about taxing your property at your death. The Artful Dodger, when feeling expansive, often gestures toward his home, Chez Dodger, and declares proudly to his son, Roger Dodger, "Someday, all of this will belong to you!" This is unfortunate not only because it is a cliché but also because it is not quite true. Although lacking in dramatic effect, it would be more literal for Art to say, "Someday, all of this will belong to you . . . and your partner, Uncle Sam."

For indeed, Uncle Sam is a silent partner who lays claim to his share of your property at death. In computing that share the first step is to determine the value of your gross estate.

Your Gross Estate

Your house, your yacht, your Nordic Track, all property you own at death is included in your gross estate.

Uncle Sam, in a rare sporting gesture, allows your representative to value your property at either the date of your death or six months later. It's a no-lose proposition since the election can be made after the six months have passed, when the values on both dates are known. For example, let's say Grandfather Cornelius's entire estate consisted of stock in Excelsior, Inc. worth $1,900,000 at his death, which declined in value to $1,600,000 six months later. Grandfather C's representative will choose to have the estate valued six months after Grandfather C's death at $1,600,000, thus saving tax on the $300,000 difference!

It is a common misconception that life insurance is not taxable at death. If Art owns a $100,000 policy of insurance on his life, naming his son, Roger, as the beneficiary, the $100,000 will be taxable in his estate at death. If, on the other hand, Roger owns the same policy on Art's life, none of the proceeds will be taxable on Art's death and Roger will receive the $100,000 tax-free.

Joint tenancy assets are included in your gross estate unless the other joint tenant contributed to the cost of the asset. For example, if Art owns a home in joint tenancy with Roger, unless Roger contributed to the cost of the home, its entire value will be included in Art's estate.

The rule is different if Art holds property in joint tenancy with his wife, Ellie. Then, only half of the property is included in his gross estate regardless of who paid for the asset. The same is true of assets held with Ellie as community property.

Your Taxable Estate

Your taxable estate is computed by subtracting from your gross estate certain deductions such as funeral expenses, administration expenses, and debts (your home mortgage, for example). The value of property passing to your spouse and to charity is also subtracted.

Your estate tax exemption is then subtracted from your taxable estate. So, in the case of Uncle Cornelius, if his gross estate were $1,600,000 and his deductions totaled $100,000, his taxable estate would be $1,500,000. After deducting his $1,500,000 exemption, his estate would just squeak by owing no estate tax.

State Inheritance Tax

No need to fret, at least for most of you. In roughly two-thirds of the states (see Appendix A), there is no state inheritance tax. These states do impose a "pickup" tax, however. Once your estate tax is computed, a portion of it is sent to your state treasurer and the balance to Uncle Sam. This sharing of revenue has no effect on the total estate tax. So it doesn't cost you anything.

The remaining states have their own varieties of estate and inheritance taxes, which, if you live there, you will just have to look up.

So much for the bird's-eye view. Now let's have a look at some of the details from the worm's vantage point and get on with the business of saving taxes.

UNCLE SAM'S WORST NIGHTMARE

*O*ne of the goals of the Artful Dodger, of course, is to provide for his wife, Ellie, at his death. Uncle Sam assists this goal by allowing Art to make tax-free gifts of any size to Ellie during life or at death. This is known as the unlimited marital deduction.

Art must keep one important limitation in mind, however, if he wants the gift to be tax-free. The gift to Ellie must be unconditional, that is, with no strings attached. For example, even if Art has visions of Ellie lavishing his hard-earned money on her new husband, he can't make a gift to her that is conditional on her remaining single and still get the deduction.

This requirement of an unconditional gift once created problems for many taxpayers like Art. For if Art leaves his property to Ellie outright, Ellie, at her death, just might bequeath what's left of Art's estate to her new dramatically younger husband. If on the other hand Art makes the gift conditional, it will not qualify for the unlimited marital deduction and, at Art's death, Ellie will pay tax on everything over $1,500,000. Enter the QTIP trust.

The QTIP Trust

In an attempt to solve this problem, Uncle Sam, in 1981, created the QTIP trust. (Believe me, you don't want to know what QTIP stands for. But if you insist, it stands for "qualified terminable interest property.") Now Art can leave his property to a QTIP trust for the benefit of Ellie and have it qualify for the marital deduction. Ellie must have the right to receive all trust income and to require the trustee to invest in assets that produce a reasonable return. Art can also give Ellie the right to receive support from the trust over and above the income. In fact, Art can name Ellie to act as her own trustee.

On Ellie's death, however, Art can direct that what's left in the QTIP trust will pass to his son, Roger, or to Roger's children. Ellie's widower will be out of luck. The assets of the QTIP trust will be included in Ellie's estate for estate tax purposes. But any tax generated by the QTIP trust will be paid by Roger and the little Dodgers.

The Qualified Domestic Trust

After Uncle Sam gave us the unlimited marital deduction, he started having recurring nightmares. He dreamed of the millionaire who dies leaving all of his money, tax-free, to his wife, who happens to be a citizen of Baritaria. The bereaved widow takes her entire inheritance back to her native Baritaria. On her death it is the king of Baritaria, not Uncle Sam, who collects death taxes. (At this point Uncle Sam would wake up sweaty and nearly hysterical.)

Uncle Sam created the qualified domestic trust (or QDOT) to ensure that gifts to noncitizens stayed in the United States where they eventually could be taxed. If either you or your spouse is not a U.S. citizen, you must pay close attention to what follows. Otherwise you can now skip directly to the next chapter.

If your spouse is not a citizen, and you leave him or her an amount equal to the estate exemption or less, it doesn't matter, since your gift will be protected by your exemption. If you leave your spouse more, the excess will not qualify for the marital deduction, and hence will be subject to tax, unless it passes to a qualified domestic trust. This trust can be set up by you as part of your estate plan or by your spouse within nine months of your death. The most significant features of this trust are that one of the trustees must be a U.S. citizen and, except in cases of hardship, estate taxes must be withheld if distributions of trust principal are made to your spouse. (Distributions of trust income, however, are not subject to estate tax.)

On your spouse's death, since the qualified domestic trust is in the United States rather than, for example, Baritaria, Uncle Sam finally gets to collect the estate tax. As in the case of the QTIP trust, the assets of the qualified domestic trust are included in your spouse's taxable estate. Estate taxes generated by the assets are paid by the qualified domestic trust, however, not by your spouse's beneficiaries. (Uncle Sam has warned us that all these QDOT rules will change in 2009, but let's not worry about it until then.)

Did you know that many married couples waste one of their exemptions? If you do not want the dubious distinction of being a member of this class, read on.

GETTING TWO EXEMPTIONS
FOR THE PRICE OF ONE

*E*state planning would be a simple matter if all the Artful Dodger had to do was write a will leaving his property to his wife, Ellie. If the gift to Ellie was outright or to a QTIP trust, Ellie would pay no estate taxes on Art's death. But Art might be creating problems down the road.

Let's assume Art leaves $2,000,000 to Ellie. At Art's death, due to the unlimited marital deduction, this gift will pass to Ellie tax-free. So far so good. Now assume Ellie bequeaths $2,500,000 (consisting of the money Art left her plus $500,000 of her own money) to the Dodgers' child, Roger.

Here's the rub. The bequest to Roger is not protected by the unlimited marital deduction. It is, therefore, taxable. After deducting Ellie's $1,500,000 exemption, Roger will pay estate tax on the remaining $1,000,000 in the amount of $465,000.

Somehow Art's $1,500,000 exemption got lost in the shuffle. Is there any way to avoid this nasty result? Yes, and here's how.

The Bypass Trust

This time let's assume that instead of leaving the entire $2,000,000 to Ellie outright, Art places $1,500,000 (or the estate tax exemption in the year of his death) in a bypass trust. (It is called a bypass trust because on Ellie's death the property bypasses being taxed in her estate.) Art gives the remaining $500,000 to Ellie (or to a QTIP trust). The $1,500,000 does not qualify for the marital deduction, but it is protected by Art's exemption and so passes to the bypass trust free of tax. The $500,000 does qualify for the marital deduction so it also passes to Ellie tax-free.

Now, at Ellie's death $1,000,000 (consisting of her own $500,000 and the $500,000 Art gave her) is not taxed because it is protected by Ellie's exemption. And the $1,500,000 Art put in the bypass trust is not taxed either, because since Ellie didn't own it, it is not part of her estate. Instead of paying $465,000 in estate taxes, Roger inherits $2,500,000 tax-free.

Of course, Art is suspicious. "How will this bypass trust restrict Ellie's enjoyment of the property?" he asks. As it turns out, not much.

Art can give Ellie one or more of these rights and still keep the property out of her estate:

1. The right to receive all the income from the trust.
2. The right to receive from the trust whatever amounts are necessary for her reasonable support.
3. The right to take out 5% of the value of the trust each year with no questions asked.
4. The right to choose which children or grandchildren will inherit the property at Ellie's death.

Art can even avoid trustee's fees by naming Ellie as her own trustee.

You think I'm not aware that your eyes are starting to glaze over? This is the toughest stuff you will have to learn, so don't be discouraged. To help you through this labyrinth, I have prepared two charts (Appendix B) to show you just how all this fits together.

Balancing the Estates

When one spouse has more assets than the other, it is possible to lose part of the combined $3,000,000 exemption of both spouses. Let me explain. Assume Art owns property worth $2,000,000 and Ellie owns property worth $500,000. If Art dies first, no problem (at least from the standpoint of saving taxes). Art can put $1,500,000 in the bypass trust and give $500,000 outright (or in a QTIP trust) to Ellie. At Ellie's death both the bypass trust and what's left in Ellie's estate (up to the amount of her exemption) will pass to Roger tax-free.

But if Ellie dies first, since she has only $500,000 to put in the bypass trust, part of her $1,500,000 estate tax exemption will be wasted. At Art's death, Ellie's bypass trust containing $500,000 will avoid tax, but Roger will pay tax on the remaining $500,000 in Art's estate that is not protected by Art's $1,500,000 exemption.

One solution is for Art to make a lifetime gift to Ellie of $500,000, thereby balancing both estates. Then no matter who dies first, neither spouse's exemption will be wasted. Art must realize, of course, that the gift is irrevocable such that no matter what the future brings, he can never get it back.

Overfunding the Bypass Trust

Now I am going to make a really shocking suggestion. Let's assume Ellie has assets worth $5,000,000 instead of $500,000. What if at Art's death, Art's representative (who is probably Ellie) puts $2,000,000 instead of $1,500,000 into the bypass trust? True, Art's exemption protects only $1,500,000 so Ellie will pay estate tax on the extra $500,000. But the tax will start out at the lowest rate (45%). At Ellie's death that $500,000 (less $225,000 of estate taxes paid at Art's death) plus any appreciation during Ellie's remaining life will avoid being taxed at Ellie's higher rate of 48%.

As the estate tax exemption goes up and the tax rates come down, this technique will gradually lose its appeal. Besides, most of us are not too keen on the idea of incurring a tax now, even at lower rates, that can be delayed until our death.

Now it's time for a real-life case history to see how the QTIP and the bypass trusts work hand in hand to save taxes. So "no clicking," stay right here.

PUTTING IT ALL TOGETHER

ederal law requires the following consumer protection warning: "It has been determined that this chapter is uncommonly tiresome. Do not read this chapter while operating a motor vehicle."

The Two-Trust Plan

Let's see how the QTIP and bypass trusts can be used in setting up a tax-efficient estate plan for Art and Ellie. Art's will (or trust) might read something like this:

I confirm to my wife, Ellie, her one-half of our community property and all her separate property. By this will I intend to dispose of my one-half of the community property and all my separate property.

At my death my executor shall divide my estate into two trusts called the Art Dodger bypass trust and the Art Dodger QTIP trust. My executor shall put assets equal in value to my estate tax exemption (for example, $1,500,000 in 2004 and 2005) into my bypass trust and the rest of my assets into my QTIP trust (or if Ellie is not a U.S. citizen, my qualified domestic trust).

I appoint Ellie as the trustee of these trusts, but if she cannot serve, I appoint my son, Roger, as the successor trustee.

The trustee shall pay Ellie all the income from my QTIP trust at least annually and as much of the principal as is necessary for her support in accordance with her accustomed manner of living. If Ellie disclaims (see Chapter 8) any part of the QTIP trust, that part shall be added to the bypass trust.

The trustee shall also pay Ellie as much of the income or principal of the bypass trust as is necessary for her support in accordance with her accustomed standard of living. However, the trustee in making these payments should take into consideration any other assets (including Ellie's own property and the assets in my QTIP trust) available to Ellie for her support.

At Ellie's death my QTIP and bypass trusts shall be distributed to my child and grandchildren, outright or in trust, as Ellie shall appoint; however, failing such appointment, these trusts shall be distributed to my son, Roger, if he survives Ellie, and if he does not, to my grandchildren, the little Dodgers, in equal shares.

Caution: As a concession to the attention span of my readers, I have oversimplified this will. It should not be used by Art, Ellie, or any of you. You can anticipate that the Dodger's Clever Attorney (or yours) will take this simple document and, through the miracle of word processing, transform it instantly into twenty-seven pages of legal prose that will make heavy the eyelids of the most chronic insomniac.

Advantages

To summarize, this estate plan accomplishes several important goals:

- Art's exemption is preserved in the bypass trust so that at Ellie's death, the bypass trust passes to Roger tax-free.
- The QTIP trust (or the qualified domestic trust if Ellie is not a U.S. citizen) qualifies for the unlimited marital deduction and so is not taxable at Art's death.
- Art's will limits to whom both his trusts are distributed at Ellie's death to his child and grandchildren, but Ellie is given the right to redistribute both trusts among these family members as future circumstances may dictate.
- Requiring the trustee to distribute the bypass trust to Ellie only after taking into account Ellie's other resources, including the QTIP trust, saves taxes at Ellie's death, for it forces Ellie to consume the QTIP trust first (which will be taxable in her estate to the extent it is not consumed) and the bypass trust last (which will pass tax-free to Roger).
- Giving Ellie the option to disclaim the QTIP trust assets into the bypass trust allows Ellie to "overfund" the bypass trust.

She can thus choose to incur a tax at Art's death at tax rates lower than at her death.

✐ Neither trust will be subject to probate at Ellie's death, and if properly drafted neither trust will be subject to the claims of Ellie's creditors.

So, as you can see, these trusts are pretty hot stuff. But Ellie must pay careful attention to what she is doing as trustee of these trusts, or she could end up in some pretty hot water.

THE TRUSTEE TRAP

*L*ike the ghost of Christmas future, let me transport you to a time twenty years hence. Art has died, and Ellie now finds herself as the trustee of these wonderful tax-saving trusts we've been talking about. Fortunately, the Clever Attorney, although more long-winded and suffering from a bit of short-term memory loss, still can be relied on for sound advice.

Thank goodness, because too often attorneys fail to warn surviving spouses of some dangerous pitfalls that await the unsuspecting trustee. These pitfalls are more perilous (1) in situations where the ultimate beneficiaries of the trust are not the children of the trustee or (2) in cases of family discord. To give this narrative some much-needed dramatic tension, we will assume that Ellie and Roger are not on friendly terms. Therefore, the Clever Attorney advises Ellie that she must toe the line.

Fiduciary Duty

As trustee, Ellie has a fiduciary (derived from the Latin "fido," meaning loyal cartoon dog) duty toward Roger and the little Dodgers, who are the ultimate beneficiaries of the trusts. This is the highest duty imposed by the law, so Ellie must take this responsibility seriously. This duty includes . . .

The Duty of Impartiality

Ellie cannot favor one beneficiary (i.e., herself) over another (i.e., Roger). For example, assuming Ellie has no assets of her own, how much can she pay herself from Art's trusts for her support? Can she take a cruise? If so, can she travel first class or must she go steerage? Can she eat caviar or must she eat rattrap cheese? No matter how much or how little Ellie takes out of Art's trusts, Roger no doubt will consider it excessive, for every penny Ellie takes out is a penny less that Roger will eventually receive.

The Duty to Account

Ellie must prepare periodic accountings detailing such things as income, expenses, gains, and losses on sales of assets, etc. This requires basic accounting skills and knowledge of the Principal and Income Act. Ellie must also file income tax returns for Art's trusts. In short, Ellie had better retain the services of a Clever Accountant to help her in these complex matters.

The Duty Not to Self-Deal

Ellie must take special care in situations in which her personal interests may be (or may appear to be) in conflict with those of the trusts. Let's say one of Art's trusts owns one-half of the Dodgers' residence and Ellie owns the other. Ellie wants to buy out the trust's one-half so she can own 100% of the residence. Even if Ellie pays a fair price for the home, Roger can void the transaction on the basis that Ellie as trustee violated her fiduciary duty by dealing with herself.

The Duty to Make Property Productive

As trustee Ellie has the duty to invest trust assets prudently. Many states have passed laws setting out investment standards that trustees must follow. For example, in most states Ellie has a duty to diversify trust investments. She must also protect Roger's interests from inflationary devaluation by investing for growth as well as income. Unless Ellie is an expert herself, she should seek investment assistance from a professional.

The Duty to Keep Trusts Separate

Art's bypass trust will pass to Roger tax-free, but Art's QTIP trust will be taxable in Ellie's estate. Therefore, Ellie must keep the two trusts separate, that is, separate accounts, separate tax identification numbers, and separate tax returns. For if she doesn't, Uncle Sam will tax the bypass trust in Ellie's estate and less will pass to Roger (which, in view of Roger's shabby behavior, may not be such a bad result).

How to Make It Better

Obviously, the last thing Art intended was that his inspired estate plan would result in Ellie and Roger at each other's throats. Art could have prevented some problems by stating his intentions more specifically in his will. For example, if he wanted Ellie to have more flexibility in making distributions of support to herself, he could have stated that his primary objective was the welfare of Ellie and that "support" should be liberally construed in her favor. Or if Art felt that no words would be sufficient to prevent internecine bloodshed, he could have named a bank as trustee rather than Ellie. Corporate trustees, although they charge roughly 1% of the value of the trust annually, can be invaluable in preserving harmonious family relationships (or, in extreme cases, preventing murder).

Finally, Ellie can sidestep most of the pitfalls by seeking the assistance of the court. For example, before Ellie purchases the residence from Art's trust, she can file a petition seeking court approval. At the hearing, the judge will make an order after considering the positions of all beneficiaries. If the court decides in Ellie's favor, she can purchase the residence without fearing a sniper attack from Roger.

Time to wake up back in the present and take a look at an often overlooked way to save your grandchildren lots of taxes.

PASSING WEALTH TAX-FREE TO YOUR GRANDCHILDREN

efore we go any further, I must lay to rest a persistent rumor. This book is not about to be made into a major motion picture starring Clint Eastwood as the unlimited marital deduction. Now that we've scotched this bit of gossip, let's get back to the business of saving taxes.

The planning techniques we have discussed so far have been aimed at saving your spouse and your children taxes. Some of you may want to take the longer view and look at ways to save your grandchildren taxes as well.

Taxing Each Generation

Let's again turn to our favorite taxpayers to help illustrate. The Dodgers' son, Roger, as we know, has six children. Roger has made a fortune speculating in pork bellies. When the Dodgers leave their money to Roger, it will be taxed in the estate of either Art or Ellie, whoever dies last. Since Roger is already wealthy, he may not spend his inheritance. Therefore, at Roger's death what's left of his parents' money will be taxed again in his estate before passing to his children.

It occurs to Art, who although avaricious is not so dumb, that this double estate tax could be avoided if he gave his money directly to his grandchildren (Roger's children). In this way Art's money would not be taxed in Roger's estate but would pass directly to the little Dodgers.

For many years Art's idea worked. Taxpayers gave as much money as they wanted to their grandchildren so the money would escape being taxed in the estates of their children. Gifts of this type came to be known as generation-skipping transfers.

Uncle Sam finally said "enough is enough" and in 1976 made his first attempt to limit generation-skipping transfers.

The Grandchild's Exemption

Each of us has a grandchild's exemption. (In truth, this sobriquet is a tad misleading. This exemption applies to transfers not only to your grandchildren, but also to your nieces and nephews, and to any other beneficiaries more than one generation younger than you.)

This exemption started out being equal to $1,000,000 until 1998, when it started increasing by inflation in $10,000 increments. Nowadays, however, it is simply the same as the estate tax exemption so that in 2004 it is equal to $1,500,000, increasing to $3,000,000 in 2009. For the purposes of this chapter we will assume it is equal to $1,500,000.

What all this means is that Art can leave $1,500,000 (in 2004–2005) to his grandchildren. Just like in the good old days, this $1,500,000 will not be taxed in Roger's estate. But Uncle Sam taxes gifts in excess of $1,500,000 to grandchildren with a vengeance. Not only will Art's estate be taxed on the amount of any gift to the little Dodgers in excess of $1,500,000, but Uncle Sam also adds on a rapacious generation-skipping penalty, which is due nine months after Art's death.

The trick is to limit generation-skipping transfers to $1,500,000 and not a penny more. So Art and Ellie must content themselves with each giving no more than $1,500,000 ($3,000,000 in all) to their grandchildren.

The Generation-Skipping Trust

Since money won speculating in pork bellies can be lost speculating in pork bellies, Art is worried that Roger may need the $1,500,000 after all. No problem. Instead of leaving $1,500,000 outright to his grandchildren, Art can leave the money, in trust, to Roger for Roger's life, with the balance passing to the little Dodgers at Roger's death. Roger can even be his own trustee.

If Roger needs the money, he can withdraw what he reasonably requires for his living expenses. Or Roger can leave the money in the trust and watch it grow. Of course, the income earned by the trust is taxed each year. But at Roger's death whatever is left in the trust will pass to the little Dodgers without being taxed in Roger's estate—hence the name, generation-skipping trust.

The potential tax savings are pretty heady stuff. Let's assume Roger survives his dad by twenty years and that money invested wisely doubles every ten years. At Roger's death, Art's $1,500,000 will have increased to $6,000,000, and the entire $6,000,000 will pass to the little Dodgers without being taxed in Roger's estate.

Ellie can do the same thing, which will pass twice as much, tax-free, to the little Dodgers. In fact, Art and Ellie can first each leave $1,500,000 to a trust for the other's benefit. Thus, only at the death of the survivor will the $3,000,000 pass into Roger's trust.

To illustrate this technique (and because I have recently become quite good at making boxes and lines on my word processor), I have prepared a chart for you (Appendix C).

Balancing the Estates

Remember in Chapter 4 how a gift from Art to Ellie avoided wasting Ellie's estate tax exemption? Good! Because the same technique applies to generation-skipping transfers.

Assume Art has separate property worth over $3,000,000 and Ellie has nothing. If Art dies first, he can leave his estate to Ellie in such a way that both his and Ellie's grandchild's exemption are fully used so that a total of $3,000,000 (plus appreciation) will pass to the little Dodgers without being taxed in Roger's estate.

But if Ellie dies first, her exemption will be lost and only $1,500,000 (plus appreciation) can pass to the little Dodgers tax-free. After consulting independent legal counsel, Art may decide to make a lifetime gift to Ellie of $1,500,000, thereby assuring that both grandchild's exemptions will be fully utilized regardless of who dies first.

As the estate tax exemption continues to increase, generation-skipping planning will be useful to fewer and fewer of us. For the very wealthy, however, it may continue to provide dramatic tax savings so long as estate taxes are with us.

In the next chapter, Art's ship finally comes in. But, alas, too late.

THANKS, BUT NO THANKS

Last week the Artful Dodger's ship finally came in. Art's Aunt Agatha died at the age of ninety-two and left him a tidy sum. Years ago this would have been cause for celebration (after Art had worked through his grief, of course). But now, Art doesn't need the money. The inheritance will only increase the size of Art's estate and push him into a higher estate tax bracket.

Too Much, Too Late

Fortunately, Art has never been one to hold things in. And one evening at the local watering hole, Mac's Tea Room, Art complained to his Clever Attorney about his ship that came too late. Art's Clever Attorney suggested that Art drop in the next morning with a copy of Aunt Agatha's will to see if anything could be done.

Aunt Agatha's will contained the following gift to Art: "To my tightwad nephew, Artful Dodger, I give the sum of $100,000, if he survives me, and if he does not, I give this sum to his son, Roger."

The Solution

Art's Clever Attorney explained that the solution to Art's problem was for Art to disclaim the $100,000 gift. A disclaimer is a legal way of saying "Thanks, but no thanks." If Art disclaims the gift, the $100,000 will pass to Roger as if Art had died before his aunt. This is a once-in-a-lifetime opportunity for Art to make a tax-free gift to Roger without using up any of his exemption.

The Technical Stuff

Not surprisingly, however, Uncle Sam has established some strict requirements for disclaimers:

1. Art's disclaimer must be in writing.
2. Art must make the disclaimer within nine months of Aunt Agatha's death.
3. Art cannot receive any benefits from the gift. For example, if Art had received the interest from the $100,000, he would be out of luck.
4. Art cannot direct where the gift goes. But Aunt Agatha can. She has named Art's son, Roger, to receive the $100,000 if Art dies before her. Therefore, the gift will pass to Roger, if Art disclaims, without any direction from Art.
5. The disclaimer must be irrevocable. Once the disclaimer is filed with the probate court,

> *Nor all your piety,*
> *nor wit shall lure it back*
> *to cancel half a line;*
> *nor all your tears*
> *wash out a word of it.*

So Art must reflect seriously on what he is about to do.

Art, upon reflection, decides it would be nice, after all, to have, say, $25,000 to take his wife, Ellie, on a long-promised cruise. No problem. Art can disclaim only $75,000 and keep the balance.

A Word of Caution

However, there is a flaw in the ointment (as Mrs. Malaprop would say). Remember the generation-skipping tax we talked about in the last chapter? Of course you do! Well, if Art makes a disclaimer, it's as if the gift passed directly from Aunt Agatha to Roger. Since Roger is more than one generation below Aunt Agatha, the gift could be subject to the confiscatory generation-skipping tax if Aunt Agatha has already used up her grandchild's exemption. Before making the disclaimer, Art should talk to Aunt Agatha's attorney to make sure he is not walking into a tax trap.

Other Uses of Disclaimers

As we will see in future chapters, disclaimers can also be used to reassign benefits payable from insurance policies, annuities, or retirement accounts. For example, Art can name Ellie as the primary beneficiary of his life insurance with his bypass trust as the first contingent beneficiary and Roger as the second contingent beneficiary. If, at Art's death, Art's estate is not large enough to fill up the bypass trust, Ellie can disclaim her rights as beneficiary and the insurance proceeds will flow into the bypass trust to the extent needed to top it off to $1,500,000 (or the applicable exemption amount). If, on the other hand, neither Ellie nor the bypass trust needs the proceeds, Ellie can disclaim her rights as the primary beneficiary of the bypass trust and the proceeds will pass to Roger.

Next we'll look at one of the simplest tax-saving devices that over time can yield huge rewards.

THE MOUSE THAT ROARED

Most of you probably know that every year you can give away $11,000 to each of any number of people tax-free. (This $11,000 periodically increases for inflation in $1,000 increments. So by the time you have bought this book, it may be higher.) What you may not fully appreciate is the magnitude of the tax savings that can be achieved by this simple device. This so-called annual exclusion is truly the mouse that roared.

For example, take our friend, the Artful Dodger. Art can give $11,000 to his son, Roger, and each of the six little Dodgers ($77,000 in all) each calendar year tax-free. If Art's wife, Ellie, joins in the gift, together they can give $154,000.

In just a few years Art and Ellie can give away substantial sums of money that might otherwise be taxed at their deaths.

There is one important restriction. The gifts must be of a present interest to qualify for the annual exclusion. In other words, the gifts must have no strings attached. Art will be quick to point out that one of his grandchildren is only fourteen. He is understandably reluctant to give $11,000 to a teenager who is likely to turn around and "invest" the money in the most expensive dirt bike in the county.

The Minor's Trust

Uncle Sam, who, for all we know, may have grandchildren of his own, has tried to solve Art's problem by creating what's known as the minor's trust. Art can give $11,000 each year to a trust for the benefit of each minor grandchild, and the gift will qualify for the $11,000 annual exclusion. Uncle Sam insists that the trust money be available for the benefit of the child until he or she reaches age twenty-one, at which time the money must be payable to the child upon demand. Moreover, if the child dies before reaching age twenty-one, the money is included in the minor's estate.

The Uniform Transfers to Minors Act

Uncle Sam also allows for tax-free gifts to minors under the Uniform Transfers to Minors Act, which most states have adopted. As in the case of the minor's trust, the money must be paid to the child at age twenty-one (age twenty-five, if the gift is made at Art's death). The advantage of this type of gift is that it usually can be accomplished without the benefit of high-priced legal talent.

A Crummey Trust

In a famous tax case, a taxpayer by the name of Mr. Crummey (no kidding, that was his real name) was not satisfied with either of these two options. He was horrified at the thought of his children getting their hands on the trust money at age twenty-one. So Mr. Crummey and his Clever Attorney drafted a different kind of trust.

It provided that when Mr. Crummey transferred $10,000 (the old exclusion amount) to a child's trust, the child had the right to take the $10,000 out the same year, thus satisfying the requirement that the gift be of a present interest. If the child failed to do so, the money would remain in the trust until the child was thirty-five. (Mr. Crummey could have chosen any age.) Mr. Crummey never intended that a child exercise his or her right of withdrawal. And since Mr. Crummey could disinherit any child who did, it's a good bet that Mr. Crummey got his way.

Mr. Crummey's trust has been upheld by the courts and is now a popular estate-planning device. You can hardly blame attorneys for preferring the minor's trust, however. For it can hardly be good for business to have a client running around town telling all his friends that his attorney drafted a "Crummey trust."

The "Empowered" Crummey

For more than twenty years, Mr. Crummey hogged the legal limelight as the popularity of his trust increased. Then along came Ms. Cristofani.

She wanted to make annual exclusion gifts to her children and grand-children but she wanted her children to have the enjoyment of the entire trust property during their lifetimes, with the trust passing to the grandchildren only on the death of her children. So Ms. Cristofani had her Clever Attorney draft a trust that did just that.

Uncle Sam, who liked the Crummey trust not a dime's worth, went fruitcake over this "empowered" Crummey. And no wonder, for it gives taxpayers such as the Dodgers a new way to save taxes.

For example, each year Art and Ellie can give $154,000 (7 × $22,000) to Roger and the six little Dodgers in trust. Roger and each of the little Dodgers must be given the right to withdraw $22,000 during the year of the gift. And, voilà, a perfect trust every time! For it achieves the following:

- The gift is tax-free;
- Roger is the lifetime beneficiary of the entire trust;
- On Roger's death, the property passes to the little Dodgers free of any tax in Roger's estate; and
- None of Art's or Ellie's grandchild's exemption is used up.

Uncle Sam's continuing fulminations so far have been in vain, and the Cristofani trust is gaining acceptance as a valuable planning tool.

The Qualified State Tuition Program

Having been unsuccessful in sidetracking either the Crummey or the Cristofani trust, Uncle Sam tried a new tack. He set about inventing his own trust, known as the Qualified State Tuition Program, which he tried to make even better than either the Crummey or the Cristofani trust. Under this program Art, for example, can contribute $11,000 each year into an educational fund for each of the little Dodgers. "So what's the big deal?" you ask. The big deal is that:

- The money grows tax-free—the gains are taxed to the little Dodgers only when they spend it, except that withdrawals for educational purposes are exempt from income tax.
- Art can change the beneficiary from one little Dodger to another.

✒ Art can even take the money back (but he will incur a penalty, probably 10%, if he does).

✒ If Art contributes $55,000 in one year to an educational fund for one of the little Dodgers, Uncle Sam will average the gift over five years as if Art had contributed $11,000 in each of the five years.

✒ There are no age limitations—Art can set up an educational trust for his ancient ancestor, Aunt Agnes.

In the next chapter we will look at gifts of different sizes, at least one of which is guaranteed to fit.

GIFTS IN THREE DIFFERENT SIZES

M̲aking gifts, especially to family members, is one of the most effective ways to save estate taxes. Since the Artful Dodger's path to earthly bliss is through tax avoidance, he is anxious to learn all he can about gifts, which, as it turns out, come in three convenient sizes—small, medium, and large.

Annual Exclusion Gifts

As you know, each calendar year Art can give $11,000 to his son, Roger, and to each of Roger's six children tax-free (or to anyone else, for that matter). Art and his wife, Ellie, together can give twice this amount. What you may not know is that Art can also pay the medical expenses and tuition of Roger and his children. For these gifts to be tax-free, however, Art must pay the money directly to the medical care provider or the educational institution.

But what if Art becomes incompetent and loses the capacity to make a gift? On the advice of his Clever Attorney, Art has executed a Durable General Power of Attorney (see Chapter 23) giving his agent the power to make annual exclusion gifts to family members. If Art becomes incompetent, his trustee (probably Ellie) can continue to pay $11,000 each year to each of the little Dodgers on Art's behalf.

Gifts Protected by the Exemption

Like every other taxpayer, Art was born with a belly button and a gift tax exemption. This means Art can give away during his life a total of $1,000,000 tax-free. (Unlike the estate tax exemption, this amount does not increase over time.) Art used to view this exemption much as a squirrel views nuts stored for the winter. The last thing he wanted to do was to consume it. After a chat with his Clever Attorney, however, Art had a change of heart.

For example, Art owns a summer cabin on Silver Slough worth $150,000. If Art gives the cabin to Roger, he will use up $150,000 of his exemption, true. But the cabin plus any increase in its value will be removed from Art's estate. If the cabin appreciates $100,000 between the date of the gift and the date of Art's death, estate taxes on this $100,000 will have been saved.

Gifts in Excess of the Exemption

Art was so impressed with his Clever Attorney's advice that he used up his entire $1,000,000 exemption by making gifts to Roger and the little Dodgers. Believe it or not, from now on, Art can make additional gifts at a bargain price. Let me explain.

To make it simple, let's assume Art is in a 45% estate and gift tax bracket. If Art gives Roger $100,000, he will have to pay a gift tax of $45,000. It will, therefore, cost Art $145,000 to make a $100,000 gift. If Art doesn't make the gift but, instead, leaves Roger $145,000 in his will, at Art's death estate taxes of $65,200 (45% of $145,000) will be deducted from Roger's bequest. In other words, it will cost $145,000 to make a $79,750 bequest.

How can this be? I told you earlier that tax rates for gifts and estates are the same. This is the truth, but it's not the whole truth. Uncle Sam doesn't tax the tax on gifts. But he does tax the tax on estates. As a result, it is one-third cheaper to give your estate away during your life than at death.

Be Careful!

Art must take something very important into account before making a gift. Let's return to Silver Slough. Art paid $10,000 for the cabin many years ago. (We call this $10,000 Art's tax basis.) If Art gives Silver Slough to Roger, Roger will take over Art's $10,000 tax basis. If Roger sells the cabin for $250,000, he will pay capital gains tax on $240,000 (the difference between the sales price of $250,000 and the tax basis of $10,000).

If, on the other hand, Art bequeaths Silver Slough to Roger, Roger will receive a new tax basis equal to the value of the cabin at Art's death, say $250,000. If Roger sells the cabin for $250,000, he will pay no capital gains tax.

The solution is for Art to give Roger assets that have not appreciated (such as cash, bonds, or his Enron stock) or assets that Roger is not likely to sell during his lifetime (such as the summer cabin). Likewise, Art should hold on to assets that have gone up in value.

As a final caution, before making any large gifts to Roger, Art should dust off Shakespeare's Collected Works and reread *King Lear*.

As a lad, Uncle Sam napped through Euclidian geometry. We'll see next just how this can work to your advantage.

NON-EUCLIDIAN GIFTS

ncle Sam has some rather embarrassing gaps in his formal education, geometry being one. (In fact, if the truth be known, Uncle Sam thinks Euclid refers to a tribe of North American Eskimos.) Therefore, he never grasped the basic Euclidian hypothesis that the whole is equal to the sum of its parts. Uncle Sam's loss can be your gain, especially when it comes to making annual exclusion gifts of large assets, such as the family business or a vacation home, to younger generations. Allow me to explain.

Let's assume Art and Ellie own a business that has recently been appraised at $220,000. The Dodgers want to transfer the business to Roger so it will not be taxed in their estate. As I hope you know by now, Art and Ellie can give Roger $22,000 each year tax-free. Your lightning mathematical sense no doubt tells you the Dodgers can give Roger only 10% of the business in the first year. Your lightning mathematical sense is wrong.

Minority Discount

Remarkably, Uncle Sam allows the value of a minority interest to be discounted. The theory is that the minority interest is worth less because it is subject to the control of the majority owners. This is true even if the majority owners, to wit: Art and Ellie, happen to be the parents of the minority owner, to wit: Roger.

How much less? That is for an appraiser to determine. A 20% discount for a minority interest is not unusual. In that case, the Dodgers could give more than 10% of the business to Roger the first year and still be within their $22,000 annual exclusion. And that's not all.

Marketability Discount

As in many families, there is a certain amount of friction between Ellie and her daughter-in-law, Thelma (Roger's wife). In fact, Ellie has mentioned with great feeling (not to mention alliteration) that she would "first fry in hell" before letting Thelma get her "fat little fingers" in the family business. Therefore, the Dodgers have asked their Clever Attorney to draft an agreement giving them the right to buy back Roger's interest at a set price if he dies before they do. This buy–sell agreement eliminates the risk that Thelma will get involved in the business. It also further reduces the value of the gift to Roger, since this restriction makes Roger's interest less marketable. This in turn allows the Dodgers to give Roger an even greater percentage of the business and still stay within their $22,000 annual exclusion.

The Entity

The form of the Dodgers' business is important. For example, if the business is conducted as a general partnership, the gift to Roger will make him a general partner. As such he will have unlimited personal liability for partnership debts. Roger may be reluctant to accept this risk. Roger will also have a voice in the management of the business. Art may be unwilling to accept this risk.

If the business is a limited partnership and Art is the general partner, by law Roger can have no management authority. If the business is a corporation, Art can limit Roger's authority by giving him only nonvoting stock. In both cases, and in the case of a limited liability company as well, Roger's liability will be limited to the value of his investment.

Discounts aren't limited to business entities. They apply as well to many other assets such as the real estate investments or the summer cabin on Silver Slough.

In the next chapter I'm going to reveal something very personal about Uncle Sam that may shock you. It may also save you taxes.

GAMBLING WITH UNCLE SAM

Wou may find this hard to believe, but Uncle Sam is an incurable gambler. (Remember, you read it here first.) He has joined Gamblers Anonymous and tried numerous expensive cures (all at taxpayer expense), but to no avail. Fortunately, taxpayers can sometimes win bets with Uncle Sam. So if you, too, occasionally like to "play the ponies," pay close attention to what I'm about to tell you.

Several years ago, just when it appeared Uncle Sam had finally kicked the habit, he fell off the wagon with a thud and offered taxpayers a betting proposition that many found irresistible. Of course, the Artful Dodger jumped at the chance to win a nickel off Uncle Sam. Here's how.

The Proposition

Art's residence, Chez Dodger, is worth $500,000. If Art leaves the residence to his son, Roger, it will be taxed in Art's estate when he dies. Instead of leaving the residence to Roger, Uncle Sam allows Art to transfer the residence into a qualified personal residence trust (known by tax experts and in gambling circles as a QPRT). Art gets to live in the residence for as many years as he chooses. Let's say Art chooses eight years. After eight years, the trust terminates, and ownership of the residence must pass to Roger.

Here's the gamble: Assuming Art is age 65 when he establishes the QPRT, if he lives eight years or more he wins. Art has made a gift to Roger of the residence, but the value of the gift is discounted to $395,000 to take into account the eight years Art can continue to live there. (This value will vary depending on the interest rate used by

Uncle Sam, which changes monthly. For this example, I have used 6%.) Sure, Art has used up $395,000 of his exemption. But in return he has removed a $500,000 residence, plus any appreciation occurring after the gift, from his taxable estate.

If Art doesn't survive the eight years, Uncle Sam wins. The residence falls back into Art's estate where it is taxed at 100% of its value on the date of Art's death. It's as if the QPRT had never existed.

The trick, obviously, is for Art to guess right in choosing the number of years he will survive. The more years he chooses, the greater the discount. For example, if Art had chosen ten years, the gift would have been valued at $212,240. If Art gets too piggy, however, and picks fifteen years the gift value is $123,535, but if he doesn't survive that long, he will lose his bet with Uncle Sam and the whole scheme will go for naught.

Some Details

Art, always the skeptic, has a number of questions:

What if I survive the eight years but don't want to leave my residence?

In that case, Art can continue to live in the residence as long as he is willing to pay Roger a fair rent. Paying rent will further reduce Art's taxable estate. And Roger, under the implicit threat of disinheritance, will not be inclined to serve Art with a notice terminating his tenancy.

Will this plan work with any other assets?

Yes, Art can also put one other residence, such as his summer cabin, Silver Slough, into a separate qualified personal residence trust. But that's it; only two per customer.

What if I later decide to sell my residence?

The trust can sell Art's residence and reinvest the proceeds in a replacement residence. The trustee has two years, at most, however, to buy a replacement residence.

If I sell our residence, do Ellie and I still get to take advantage of our combined $500,000 homeowner's exemption?

Yes.

Can Ellie and I each transfer half of our residence or Silver Slough into a separate QPRT?

Yes, and there are several advantages to this approach. First, Art and Ellie can each pick a different term depending or their respective life expectancies. And, second, the transfers qualify for a fractional interest discount (see Chapter 11), which further reduces the value of the gift.

Are there any disadvantages to establishing a QPRT?

Yes, for if Art survives the term of the QPRT and the residence or summer cabin is transferred to Roger, Roger takes over Art's presumably low tax basis. If, on the other hand, Roger had inherited the property, he would have received a new, presumably high tax basis, equal to the property's value at Art's death.

Watch out, though! From time to time Uncle Sam threatens to do away with QPRTs, so they just might go the way of the dodo.

Next, let's see if we can apply the same concept to gifts of income-producing property.

HALFWAY HOUSE FOR BIG GIVERS

*O*nce every few months the Artful Dodger locks the door to his study, unlocks the lower left-hand desk drawer, and removes a wad of corporate bonds. Art loves these corporate bonds. He loves the heft of the scissors as they cut out the tiny coupons. He loves the engraved pictures of men with Herculean physiques holding aloft locomotives belching smoke. And those of naked goddesses (20 pounds overweight by today's standards—just right by Art's) looking imperious as lightning bolts stream from their fingertips.

What Art does not love, however, is the thought that these bonds will be taxed in his estate. True, it makes sense to give them to Roger and the little Dickens, er, Dodgers. But Art cannot bear to part with these icons of American enterprise, at least not just now.

How can Art give these bonds to his family members yet still keep them? (No, this is not one of those riddles the Elizabethans were simply wild about. There really is a way.)

The Gift with Strings

Art can give the bonds away but retain the right to receive the income from the bonds for a period of years he can choose. For example, if Art has $100,000 of Black, Inc. bonds paying 10%, he can choose to receive the stream of income from these bonds for ten years. After that, the bonds must pass, income and all, to Roger and the little Dodgers.

Actually, what Art must do is transfer his bonds into a grantor retained annuity trust (GRAT) or a grantor retained unitrust (GRUT). GRATs and GRUTs (in addition to being the most revolting acronyms you will find in this book) are sort of halfway houses for people who, like Art, are not quite ready to make an immediate gift.

A GRAT will pay Art 10% of the original value of the bonds each year for ten years. The annual payment will always be the same.

A GRUT will pay Art 10% of the value of the bonds determined each year. Therefore, the annual payment will vary depending on the fluctuations of the bond market.

The Discount

But what is the point of all this? The point is that Uncle Sam reduces the amount of the gift by the value of the income interest Art retains. Therefore, by transferring the bonds into a GRAT or a GRUT, Art uses up less of his exemption than had he made a gift of the bonds outright or died with the bonds in his estate.

For example, Uncle Sam will value $100,000 of bonds transferred to a ten-year GRAT that pays 10% at only $33,560 after deducting for Art's income interest. If Art had chosen a term of 20 years, the gift would be valued at $8,699; if he had chosen 25 years, the gift would be valued at $4,639 and Art would have transferred $100,000 out of his estate for next to nothing. (The exact value of the gift depends on an interest rate established by Uncle Sam, which changes monthly, and Art's age. In these examples, I have assumed an interest rate of 6% and Art's age to be 65.)

A Bigger Discount

Even more exciting to Art is the prospect of transferring his bed-and-breakfast, Dodger Lodge, to a GRAT or a GRUT, because the lodge produces greater cash flow than does a bond and, unlike a bond, can be expected to appreciate. The discount is bigger because the cash flow allows Art to pay himself a higher percentage each year. And any appreciation after the date of the transfer escapes tax in Art's estate.

And more exciting still, if Art transfers a fractional share of Dodger Lodge to the GRAT or GRUT, the gift will be further reduced by the minority and marketability discounts you mastered in Chapter 11.

One problem with GRATs and GRUTs is that if Art does not survive the ten years (or his chosen term), the asset will be brought back into his estate at his death and taxed as if the GRAT or GRUT had never existed.

This bit of tax exotica may not be for most folks, but for those of you who just cannot let go, it could be just the thing.

Are you charitably disposed? In tax planning, although good deeds are their own reward, Uncle Sam sweetens the pot.

DOING WELL BY
DOING GOOD

*L*ook around you. The opportunities for charitable giving are everywhere. Children are going hungry; libraries are closed on weekends; high schools are without orchestras or computer labs. Not that any of this does much to soften the obdurate heart of the Artful Dodger. But when Art considers the tax savings that can result from charitable gifts, that same heart softens ever so slightly.

Whether you are truly motivated by a desire to make this world a better place or, like Art, interested mostly in saving taxes, you should know the basics of charitable giving.

Lifetime Gifts

As you all know, charitable gifts of cash are fully deductible. The fair market value of noncash gifts is also deductible. (Certain limitations apply to so few of us that I am not going to bore you with these details.) This gives rise to opportunities in the case of appreciated assets. Take Art, for example.

Years ago Art made a killing in the stock market. In just a few years, the value of his 100 shares of Black, Inc. went from $100 to $10,000. Art has heard a rumor that Black, Inc. may soon be showing some red ink and he wants to bail out.

To buy peace at home, he also feels compelled to make a gift to Ellie's favorite charity. If he sells the stock, he will pay income tax on the gain of $9,900 (the difference between his cost and the sales price), which at Art's tax bracket of 39% (state and federal) will leave him $7,228. If he then donates this sum to charity, the tax saving on this gift will amount to only $2,819.

If, on the other hand, Art simply gives the Black, Inc. stock to Ellie's favorite charity, he will avoid paying any income tax on the gain and can deduct the entire $10,000. Art's tax saving now will be $3,900. The point is simple: If you have invested wisely (or luckily), give the asset, not the proceeds.

Gifts of Tangible Personal Property

Borne aloft on a wave of munificence (or greed, if you prefer), Art rushes to his garage and surfaces with the brass spittoon he bought at auction twenty years ago for ten bucks. It is now worth $500. How many of you think he can donate it to charity and claim a $500 deduction on his tax return? How many of you think he can't? How many of you just don't give a damn?

The answer, for those of you who do care, is maybe he can and maybe he can't. If he gives the spittoon to the local SPCA, which turns around, sells it, and spends the $500 on dog biscuits, Art can deduct only the ten bucks he originally paid. If, however, he gives it to the local historical society, which displays the spittoon as part of its collection of really repulsive nineteenth-century artifacts, Art can deduct $500. Why? Because he can deduct the value (rather than the cost) of a gift of tangible personal property only if the charity can be expected to use the item in a manner related to its function. It is tax distinctions like this that cause one to wonder if Uncle Sam isn't a roaring loony.

Gifts of Life Insurance

Art has an old $25,000 life insurance policy naming Ellie as the beneficiary. Ellie doesn't really need insurance protection anymore. If Art gives the policy to charity, he can deduct the value of the policy on his income tax return and the charity will get the proceeds at Art's death.

Ellie thinks this is a great idea since her favorite charity will eventually end up with $25,000. Art thinks it's a great idea too, because of the tax deduction and because, frankly, the insurance on his life wasn't doing him much good anyway.

And there's one more advantage. A gift of life insurance to charity increases the likelihood that, at your death, your survivors will be truly grief stricken.

Gifts at Death

The value of a bequest to charity is deductible for estate tax purposes. When Ellie and Art are both gone, Ellie wants to leave $100,000 to charity. If she is in a 45% estate tax bracket, Uncle Sam will, in effect, contribute almost half the gift.

Having whetted Art's appetites, the Clever Attorney decides the time is right to introduce Art to the sine qua non of charitable opportunities.

DOING STILL BETTER

The other day the Artful Dodger had quite a shock. His Clever Attorney suggested the possibility of Art's making a substantial gift to charity. Since Art's prior charitable generosity has been limited to buying single boxes of Girl Scout cookies, Art wondered if the suggestion might be the result of a two-martini lunch. But by the time Art's Clever Attorney had finished explaining the tax advantages of this type of charitable giving, Art's cold heart had turned downright eleemosynary.

The Problem

Art owns a rental unit worth $500,000 that he purchased for peanuts many years ago. Unfortunately, it brings in only $1,250 in monthly rent. Art wants to sell the property and invest the proceeds in investments producing a higher rate of return. After paying capital gains tax on the sale, however, Art will have only $355,000 left to invest. To add insult to injury, at Art's death the $355,000 will be taxed in Art's estate. Art's son, Roger, will end up receiving a measly $159,750.

The Charitable Solution

There is an alternative to this depressing scenario, especially if Art would prefer to see tax dollars flow to charity instead of into Uncle Sam's pocket. For Uncle Sam is uncharacteristically charitable to the taxpayer who is, himself, charitable.

Instead of selling his rental, Art can set up a charitable remainder trust. Art then transfers the rental property into the trust. When the trust sells the property, it pays no capital gains tax and the entire

$500,000 can be invested in more productive assets. Art can direct that the trustee pay him a stated amount from the trust (minimum 5%) annually. He also can direct that, at his death, the trustee continue to pay this amount to his wife, Ellie, for her life. But on Ellie's death, what's left in the trust must pass to the charity of Art's choice.

Art can choose to have the trust pay him each year 5%, for example, of the original value of the trust. This is called a charitable remainder annuity trust. Or he can choose to have the trust pay him each year 5% of the value of the trust computed annually. This is called a charitable remainder unitrust.

Until recently, Art could have extended the payout over Roger's life. But Uncle Sam has tightened the screws on charitable trusts such that now it is usually not possible to include children.

Advantages

The primary advantage of a charitable remainder trust is that Art can invest the entire sales proceeds from his rental unit for the benefit of his family without any attrition due to capital gains tax.

There are other benefits as well. Art can take a charitable deduction on his income tax return, which will shelter some of the money the trust pays him each year. The amount of the deduction depends on the value of the eventual gift to charity as computed by Uncle Sam. For example, if the trust terminates on Art's death, the deduction is bigger than if the trust continues on for Ellie's life. Likewise, the smaller the percentage payout Art chooses, the bigger the deduction. And if Art can't use up the entire deduction in one year, he can use it up over the next five years.

Also, the trust will pay no capital gains tax on the sale of the assets in which it has invested. Thus, if the trust sells Intermittent Gas and Electricity, Inc. at a gain, the entire proceeds can be reinvested.

Art is still concerned that Roger will lose some of his inheritance. No problem. Art can use some of the money he receives from the trust to buy a life insurance policy on Art's life, naming Roger as the beneficiary. In fact, Art can transfer ownership of the policy to Roger. That way, at Art's death the proceeds will not be taxable in Art's estate.

One other advantage pleases Art, although he won't admit it. He and Ellie most likely will receive immediate public recognition for their generosity. All of which is better than a few stale Girl Scout cookies.

A Thrifty Alternative

For those of you who, like Art, are not too keen on having to pay your Clever Attorney to draft a charitable remainder trust, there is a thrifty alternative. You can transfer assets into a pooled income fund without the necessity of engaging high priced legal talent.

The plan is simple. Art, for example, transfers assets to a charity and, in return, the charity agrees to pay Art for his life (or, if the Dodgers choose, for the life of Art and Ellie) the income earned by the assets. The charity puts the assets in its pooled investment fund along with contributions from other benefactors. Art can expect the income he receives to fluctuate each year depending on the performance of the fund. As in the case of a charitable remainder trust, Art avoids paying capital gains tax and gets an income tax deduction. At Art's death (or the death of Art or Ellie, whoever dies last), the charity gets what's left.

In the next chapter, I will answer the question, "Do you need a will?" (Hint: When an attorney asks this question, you can bet the farm it's purely rhetorical.)

16

TO WILL OR NOT TO WILL

o far we have discussed some pretty exotic tax-planning techniques. In this chapter, we're going back to basics. Not everybody has an estate large enough to require tax planning. (Nor does everyone, like the Artful Dodger, have a borderline personality when it comes to trying to avoid taxes.)

Let's start with the most fundamental question of all.

Do You Need a Will?
If you die without a will, you die intestate. No, this doesn't mean all your earthly booty is forfeited to the state. It means that your property passes by intestate succession. This is the law that, in effect, writes your will for you if you don't have one. It provides for the distribution of your estate to the people whom the state assumes you would have chosen. Different states have different intestacy laws.

For example, if you are married and die in a community property state, your half of the community property passes to your surviving spouse and your separate property passes to both your surviving spouse and your children. If you are single, without children, your property probably passes to your parents equally.

This may not be so bad. But it also may not be what you want. Your will (or your living trust) ensures that your property passes to the people you choose.

Who's in Charge?
In your will you can name your personal representative. This is the person who will have the responsibility of administering your estate.

And you can waive the requirement for a bond. (A bond is like an insurance policy that protects your estate if the representative disappears in your Ferrari Testarossa.)

You should waive bond if you have complete trust in your chosen representative. This is important since bonds are expensive. (The last time I checked, a bond on a $750,000 estate cost about $950 per year.)

If you die intestate, your representative will be appointed by the court, and a bond may be required even if your representative is a family member.

The choice of your representative can be important. Normally it will be a family member. However, if Thanksgiving Day in your family has come to be known as the "annual brawl," you should consider someone outside the family or even a professional representative such as a bank trust department.

Alternatives to a Will

Not all property passes by your will. For example, property held in joint tenancy passes to the surviving joint tenant outside your will. Therefore, if you hold title to Bleakacre in joint tenancy with your girlfriend, Marilyn, at your death it will pass automatically to her. (If you also have left Bleakacre in your will to your other girlfriend, Carolyn, you have set the stage for the type of nasty lawsuit that allows attorneys to send their kids to private schools.)

Retirement benefits, life insurance, and some investments (like government bonds) that are payable at your death to a person you have designated will not pass by your will. Nor will bank accounts held in trust for another nor, of course, assets held in a living trust.

So it is possible for you to direct where your property will go without having a will. This is risky, however. For if the other joint tenant of Bleakacre or the beneficiary of your life insurance dies before you (or in a common disaster with you), this property will pass by intestate succession at your death.

I don't mean to scare you, but in the next chapter there will be a test of your probate IQ.

TEST YOUR PROBATE IQ

In a recent survey, average Americans were given the following multiple-choice test:

"Probate is:

(a) A really nasty toxin.
(b) A sexually transmitted disease.
(c) The judicial process for the orderly distribution of an estate."

A majority of respondents guessed wrong and no wonder. You no doubt have heard probate talked about as if it were the fifth horseman of the apocalypse. Yet, if you're like most people, you probably don't have much of an idea just what probate is.

Nonprobate Property

For starters, the following property does not have to be probated:

(a) Property held in joint tenancy;
(b) Life insurance proceeds (unless you named your probate estate as the beneficiary);
(c) Assets, such as retirement accounts (like IRAs) and government bonds, that are payable on death to a person you name;
(d) In most states, all assets passing outright from one spouse to another; and
(e) Assets held in a living trust.

The Way It Works

The rest of your property is subject to probate. Let's take a short stroll through probate to see what it's really all about. Probate procedures differ from state to state. Generically most probates are something like this:

A probate proceeding is started by the person you named in your will as your personal representative. If you didn't get around to making a will, just about anybody can start the proceeding (even one of your creditors) but preference is given to your spouse and your relatives.

The person seeking to be your representative files a petition for probate in the Superior Court. He or she then publishes a notice in a local newspaper, which informs your creditors that they must file their claims within a stated time and informs the public of the date of the first hearing. This notice must also be sent to all the beneficiaries named in your will, as well as to your next of kin.

At the first hearing, the judge appoints the person who will have the responsibility of managing your estate. This person is called an executor if he was named in your will, or an administrator if you died without a will. (If the person is a she and you are either a Latin scholar or a snob, she is called an executrix or an administratrix.) The term "personal representative" covers both.

Unless it is challenged, the judge will admit your will to probate and order letters of administration issued to your personal representative. These letters are your representative's written authority to act for the estate. Your creditors have a limited time (often four months) from the date these letters are issued to file a claim against your estate for money due, or they will be out of luck.

This cutoff of creditors' claims is an important benefit of probate. For example, if you are a doctor, a lawyer, or other professional, malpractice claims that are not filed on time are forever barred. Moreover, your representative can choose to probate both halves of the community property, thus protecting all community property, such as the family residence, from future claims.

Just what exactly does your representative do to probate your estate? Read on, Macduff.

MORE ABOUT PROBATE

I know a lot of you readers, in a state of nail-biting anxiety, have rushed ahead to learn more about the probate process. Here, then, is the second installment.

The Inventory and Appraisal

Your personal representative's first task is to inventory the property of the estate and have it appraised, usually by the probate referee. These values are used on your estate tax return if one is required.

These values also establish the new tax basis of all estate assets. For example, the vacation cottage you purchased for $50,000 (your original tax basis) will get a new basis of $500,000, the value at the date of your death. Your beneficiaries will pay capital gains tax on only those sales proceeds over $500,000.

Simplified Procedure

It used to be that every time your representative wanted to do anything important, he or she had to go to court for authority. Now, in many states your representative takes most actions such as selling property, investing estate assets, entering into contracts, and the like without going to court. Instead, he or she needs only to notify your beneficiaries in advance of any such action. If none objects, he or she can go ahead.

Help from the Judge

Occasionally your representative may run into a problem that requires court assistance. For example, let's say your will provides, "To my good friend, Art Dodger, I leave $10,000 so he can take good care of my pit bull, Vise Grips." Unfortunately, "Visey" trotted off to his reward years ago. Art claims he should get the money, anyway. Your children, who get the rest of your estate, are adamant: "No Visey, no $10,000."

Your representative can request the court to instruct him or her just what to do. Probate judges, who handle scores of probate cases each week, are adept at solving problems such as this. And your representative, in following the judge's instruction, is protected from personal liability.

Financial Stuff

During probate your representative receives all income, pays all expenses, invests surplus cash, and generally manages your estate. He or she also files your last personal income tax returns along with your estate's income tax returns, known as fiduciary returns.

If your gross estate exceeds the amount of your estate tax exemption, your representative must also file an estate tax return within nine months of your death. After the time for filing creditors' claims has expired and after your estate tax return has been filed, your estate can be closed.

Winding Things Up

To wind things up, your representative files a petition for distribution in the probate court. Unless waived by the beneficiaries, your representative must attach an itemized accounting showing all assets at the beginning of the probate and, at its end, all income and expenses, as well as all gains and losses on sales. The tricky part, of course, is that the accounting must balance.

The representative also requests approval of his or her fees and the probate attorney's fees. Your representative and the probate attorney are each entitled to a probate fee, the amount of which varies from state to state. In California, for example, the fee on an estate of $1,000,000 is $23,000 plus 1% on anything over $1,000,000 and (I realize this is getting somewhat academic) $1/2$% on anything over $10,000,000.

Your representative, especially if a family member, will probably waive this fee. Attorney's fees also may be less than the probate fee if negotiated at the beginning of the probate proceeding.

Finally, your representative sets out how the estate will be distributed. Once this petition is approved, your representative will distribute your estate and be discharged.

In the next chapter, I will tell you something that just may help you win your next bar bet.

THE LIVING TRUST:
FACT AND FICTION

Perhaps you've seen ads similar to the one that has appeared in many newspapers, in which a self-styled "money expert" invites you to attend his "Money Power Workshop." Here he promises to show you how living trusts can "reduce or eliminate estate taxes." This is pure eyewash.

The Fiction

"Living trusts save estate taxes." Not so! No living trust has ever saved a penny of estate taxes. These money experts, along with others who make their living selling living trusts like washing detergent, often confuse the public by making this claim.

The truth is, a living trust is a valuable estate planning tool you should consider. But not for the wrong reasons.

The Fact

A living trust is a will substitute. In the typical living trust, an individual transfers all of his or her property to himself or herself as trustee of a living trust. Although a living trust does not save taxes, it does avoid probate.

Probate Fees

As you know, probate is the judicial process for the orderly distribution of an estate. The problem with probate is probate fees.

Your attorney and your personal representative are each entitled to a probate fee, which is usually set by statute in each state. The fee is often the same for each. Your personal representative, if a member of your family, will probably waive the fee. Therefore, in most cases only the attorney's fee should concern you. For example, in a $500,000 estate the attorney's fee, depending on where you live (or, actually, where you die) might range from $10,000 to $15,000. (As we will see in a few paragraphs, however, this fee is not carved in marble.)

Attorneys may also charge extraordinary fees for services that go beyond the normal probate duties. Most judges, however, are loath to allow extraordinary fees unless the attorney can make a compelling case that they are justified.

If you have a living trust, there will be no probate and, ergo, no probate fee at your death. To say a living trust avoids attorney's fees is probably an overstatement. For at your death the successor trustee you name will probably hire an attorney to assist in the administration of your trust. These fees should be significantly less, however, than in the case of a probate.

Other Advantages

In addition to probate avoidance, a living trust offers other advantages. It affords an economical alternative to a conservatorship. In the event of your future incapacity, your successor trustee, rather than a court-appointed conservator, will take over handling your affairs.

If you own real property in another state, a living trust offers a simple method of transferring the property at your death without the need for setting up a probate in a foreign state.

However, a living trust costs more than a will because it is a more complicated document and because, after executing the trust, you must transfer your assets into it.

Believe it or not, probate actually has some advantages. For example, in some cases probate affords a simpler way to transfer assets to your beneficiaries. And in some community property states your representative can protect both halves of the community property from creditors' claims that are not filed on time.

A Modest Proposal

For those who are not sure they want a living trust, there is a middle ground. In your will you can advise your personal representative that probate fees, although set by statute, are negotiable. You can instruct your personal representative to negotiate probate fees before hiring a probate attorney. You can even point out that your personal representative need not hire the attorney who drafted your will to probate your estate. In the case of a well-organized estate, your personal representative should be able to negotiate a substantial reduction of the normal probate fee.

For those inclined toward a living trust, you have some work to do. Stay tuned.

IMPLEMENTING YOUR LIVING TRUST

If Art and Ellie decide a living trust is just the thing for them, there are some steps they should take to make sure the thing actually works.

Transferring Assets into the Trust

Signing a living trust is only half the job. To avoid probate, the Dodgers must also transfer their assets into the trust. From now on the Dodgers will own their assets not as Art and Ellie Dodger, just plain folks, but as Art and Ellie Dodger, co-trustees of the Dodger living trust. (This is O.K. as far as it goes, but will probably not get them a better table at the local French restaurant.) Some assets are a little more difficult to transfer than others.

Chez Dodger

The Dodgers must sign a deed transferring their home, Chez Dodger, and any other real estate to the trust. In those states that exempt a transfer to a living trust from property tax reassessment, a form should be filed with the tax assessor claiming this exemption. Also, if Chez Dodger has a mortgage, out of an abundance of caution Art may want to check with the lender, to make sure the transfer won't trigger a payoff demand. (Although a theoretical possibility, it is a rare lender that would be so dastardly as to do this.) And finally, Art should contact his insurance agent to add the trust as an insured under the Dodgers' homeowner insurance policy.

Closely Held Businesses

If Art holds an interest in a partnership or a closely held corporation that has not yet gone bankrupt, he should make sure there are no transfer restrictions. If there are, the other partners or shareholders (who may be contemplating a living trust for themselves) will probably waive the restrictions and permit the transfer.

Stocks and Bonds

This tip alone is worth the cost of this book. There are two ways to transfer securities into a living trust: the hard way and the easy way. The hard way is to write to the transfer agent of each stock or bond requesting forms necessary to put the security into your trust. In the fullness of time, after many letters back and forth, you will eventually accomplish your goal. The easy way is to put the securities into a brokerage account, then simply change the name of the account to the trust. This takes approximately five minutes.

Heirlooms

Family heirlooms, furniture, jewelry, antiques, artwork, and the like can be transferred into your trust by a simple assignment like the one in Appendix D. Be sure the assignment includes property you own now and property you may acquire in the future.

Exceptions

Not all assets must be transferred into the living trust. For example, your retirement accounts and IRAs cannot be held by a trust. But don't worry. Since these accounts pass to your designated beneficiary, they will escape probate. Likewise, life insurance (which names a beneficiary other than your estate), joint tenancy accounts, and certain other assets that are payable on your death to a named beneficiary need not be transferred into your trust since they will avoid probate anyway.

Tax Considerations

If you were to tell Uncle Sam you had a living trust, he would probably say "Huh?" because, as you now know, living trusts have nothing to do with taxes and consequently are of no interest to Uncle Sam. This is good news in a way. Art and Ellie do not have to file a separate tax return for the trust (as long as both are alive), and they can continue to use their own social security numbers on bank and securities accounts even after they have transferred them into the trust.

Community Versus Separate Property

In community property states, most living trusts provide that transferring property into the trust will not change its character. In other words, community property will remain community property and separate property will remain separate property. Art and Ellie should identify and segregate separate and community property in the trust. This will ensure favorable tax treatment of all community property (see Chapter 25). And Art and Ellie will each continue to own and control his or her separate property.

The Pour-Over Will

Just because the Dodgers execute a living trust doesn't mean they don't need a will. Art and Ellie also should execute simple wills bequeathing their estates to their living trust. This type of will is referred to as a pour-over will because it pours over into the living trust any assets inadvertently left out. It may take a probate proceeding to accomplish this, however, so the pour-over will should be regarded as a safety net rather than an alternative to physically transferring the assets into the living trust.

The next chapter is rated X. Therefore if you are reading this aloud to impressionable young children, it should be skipped over.

THE FULL MONTY

$\mathbb{N}$ow that you know something about living trusts, some of you with prurient interests may want to actually see one in the flesh. Therefore, against the advice of my publisher's attorneys, I have included a more or less unexpurgated living trust in Appendix F.

This is the trust the Clever Attorney has developed out of long experience. It contains some provisions, not found in the form books, that have proved to be of use. In the following discussion, we will again assume that it is Art who dies before Ellie.

A Brief Refresher Course

As we discussed in earlier chapters, upon Art's death, the Dodger living trust is divided into three separate trusts: the survivor's trust that contains Ellie's property and the QTIP and bypass trusts that contain Art's property. The bypass trust holds assets equal to Art's exemption (in 2004 and 2005, $1,500,000). It will pass to Roger free of estate taxes on Ellie's death. The QTIP trust holds the rest of Art's assets. Like the bypass trust, it will not be taxed at Art's death, but unlike the bypass trust, it will be subject to tax at Ellie's death. Ellie can revoke or modify the survivor's trust without limitation and, why not, since she owns it. But Art's bypass and QTIP trusts can neither be modified nor revoked.

Changing the Guard

There may come a time when Elllie wants to step down as trustee. The trust names Roger as her successor. But, Ellie doesn't have much faith in Roger's business acumen because, as we know, Roger is a bit of a gambler who doesn't believe a stock is worth buying unless its price earnings ratio is at least three times his average golf score. Ellie can always change the trustee of her survivor's trust, but Art's trusts are not modifiable. Fortunately, the Clever Attorney has put in a provision allowing Ellie to hire or fire trustees so Ellie is free to appoint her wise Uncle Edgar to take over the reins of power for all three trusts when she steps down.

Changing the Beneficiaries

Upon Ellie's death, Art's trusts go to Roger if Roger is then living and if he is not, to the little Dodgers equally. However, Art has given Ellie the authority to change this scheme. Ellie has the right to choose who among Roger and the little Dodgers will inherit Art's property. This special power of appointment allows Ellie to adjust Art's dispositive plan as future circumstances warrant. And since she can disinherit Roger, it also increases the likelihood that Roger will be really nice to his mom! Art could have given Ellie the right to leave his property to additional beneficiaries as well, such as Roger's wife, Thelma (fat chance!). Or even charity, so Ellie, if she didn't care for the way any of her progeny were turning out, could say, "a plague on all your houses," and leave Art's trusts to her favorite charity.

Saying What You Mean

After Art's death, Ellie, as trustee, has the ability to make distributions to herself from Art's trusts for her support. The last thing Art wants is Roger popping up and claiming Ellie is looting these trusts. So Art has put in several provisions to protect Ellie. The trust makes clear that Art's primary motive in establishing his trusts is the welfare of Ellie and that the interests of Roger and the little Dodgers are subordinate to hers. Also, the trustee is not required to take into account Ellie's other assets, such as those in the survivor's trust, when making distributions to her from Art's trusts. And, finally, so long as Ellie is alive the trustee's normal duty to diversify assets does not apply to the family home or other recreational property.

On the other hand, if Ellie had been Art's second wife and if Roger had been the product of Art's first marriage, Art might want to limit distributions from his trusts to Ellie so as to preserve more of his estate for Roger. For example, he could require Ellie to exhaust her assets before being entitled to support from his trusts or, at least, require that she contribute to some extent to her own support.

The point is state clearly what you intend. That way the chance of future lawsuits will be minimized. And if things do get nasty and end up in court, the judge will be more likely to make the right decision if your trust clearly expresses your true intention.

Trustee Miscellany

The Dodger trust contains other trustee provisions that are helpful especially if the successor trustee is a family member or friend:

> The Dodger trust absolves any individual trustee of liability due to mere negligence. As we have seen (Chapter 6), being a trustee can be tricky business especially when children from prior marriages are the ultimate beneficiaries. And, let's face it, even the most well meaning trustee can make a mistake. Therefore, you may wish to limit your trustee's liability to only those acts that are intentional or reckless.

> Compensation of successor trustees should be spelled out. Corporate trustees charge a fee of approximately 1% of the value of the trust annually. Appropriate compensation for noncorporate trustees is open to question. Uncle Bert may feel awkward charging a fee and, you can be sure, the beneficiaries will expect him to work for free. But being a trustee can be a pain in the bum and, therefore, you may wish to require that Uncle Bert take a fee and you may even want to specify how much.

> Although Art and Ellie are co-trustees, there may be times when it is convenient that either have the power to act on behalf of the trust without the other. For example, if Ellie is off touring Provence with her college chums, she should be able to give Art a power of attorney to act for the trust in her absence. Or, if Art is astute in financial matters, or thinks he

is, Ellie may decide to delegate to Art the authority to make all investment decisions. The trust should therefore allow one trustee to delegate to the other trustee the exclusive power to act for the trust in specified instances.

We will now fast forward twenty years to see just how these living trusts work. Hold on to your hats!

MORTE D'ARTHUR

We will now fast forward twenty years. Art has passed on. Ellie must now undertake the administration of the living trust. If all of the Dodgers' assets have been transferred into the living trust, Ellie will never see the inside of a probate court, because no probate proceeding is necessary. If not . . .

Whoops!

What if Ellie discovers that Art never got around to transferring his stock in Black, Inc. into the trust? She has several options:

- If Black, Inc. is listed in the trust as an asset, in some states it is possible to file a simple petition with the court requesting an order transferring the stock into the trust.
- Or if the value of Black, Inc. is less than a certain amount (e.g., $100,000 in California), most states provide a simple procedure for Ellie to transfer the stock into the trust without a probate.
- If none of these procedures is available, Ellie must go through an entire probate proceeding for this one asset. This is why it is so important to be sure all assets that should be in your trust are there.

Now that Ellie has taken steps to make sure Art's trust is fully funded, there are other important matters she must attend to.

Creditors' Claims

In probate, a creditor must file its claim within a specified time. If it doesn't, its claim is cut off. It used to be there was no similar protection afforded living trusts. Now in many states Ellie has the right to publish a notice to Art's creditors in the newspaper. And just like in probate, Art's creditors (and we certainly hope the Clever Attorney is not one of them) must file claims with Ellie, as the trustee, within the time stated in the notice or the claim is barred. Even if Ellie thinks Art has no creditors, she should take advantage of this simple procedure. For if 2024 is as sue-happy an age as this one, no one, not even Art, is immune.

Notification

In some states Ellie has a duty to notify Art's heirs and the beneficiaries of his trust of his death and provide them with a copy of the trust upon request. This is true even though Ellie is the only one who has the right to receive distributions from the living trust.

Filing Estate Tax Returns

If the Dodgers have done their tax planning carefully, there will be no estate tax payable on Art's death. However, if the value of Art's property exceeds his exemption (assuming there is such a thing in the year 2024), Ellie must file an estate tax return within nine months of Art's death. Art's property must be appraised for estate tax purposes. This appraised value will also establish Ellie's new tax basis. Remember: Even though Art owned only one-half of any community property, both halves of the community will get a new tax basis. If these assets have increased in value, Ellie will pay less in capital gains taxes when she sells these assets later.

Filing Income Tax Returns

Ellie must now start reporting income generated by Art's assets on separate income tax returns. Ellie may be able to save income taxes by electing to file Art's returns on a fiscal rather than a calendar year. She should be sure to discuss this option with her accountant.

Funding the Sub-Trusts

Finally, Ellie must retain her property in the survivor's trust and divide Art's property between the QTIP and the bypass trusts. Funding these sub-trusts is technical, can be complicated, and, fortunately for you, is way beyond the purview of this little book. Suffice it to say, Ellie must get professional help from her Clever Attorney or Clever Accountant. Transferring assets into the sub-trusts is similar to the procedure she and Art went through twenty years ago when they originally transferred their assets into their living trust. From now on Ellie is trustee of not one but three trusts: Art's QTIP and bypass trusts and her survivor's trust. She must account for these trusts separately, and she must never, never mix the assets of one with another.

Next let's look inside an estate planner's toolbox where we'll find some handy little tools that will fix future problems.

YOUR ESTATE PLANNING TOOLBOX

*I*n this chapter we're going to take a break from taxes. (Buck up! We'll return to them soon enough.) Instead, I'm going to tell you about documents you may want to include in your estate plan. Think of these documents as tools in your estate planning toolbox. At least one of these tools may be just the right thing to fix a future problem.

Warning! These forms are presented by way of example only. Do not use them without the advice of your own Clever Attorney.

Health Care Directive

This document (Appendix G) allows you to appoint the person of your choice to make health care decisions for you if you are unable to do so. At the same time, you can designate that your life not be artificially prolonged if your condition is irreversible, or alternatively that every measure be undertaken to keep you alive. If you want to specify your desires regarding specific life-sustaining procedures, you can attach a Statement of Desires (Appendix H) to your durable power. You may also consent to the donation of your body parts for medical or scientific purposes.

The advantage of this document is that it invests the person of your choice with the power to monitor and control the course of your medical treatment when you can't. If there is someone to whom you are willing to delegate this authority, do it!

Directive to Physicians

This document, sometimes referred to as a living will (Appendix I), is useful if there is nobody to whom you want to delegate your health care decisions. It directs your physician to withhold life-sustaining treatment if you are in an irreversible coma.

Durable General Power of Attorney

This document appoints another person to manage your financial affairs for you. You can choose to have it take effect immediately or only in the event of your future incompetency (Appendix J). In cases of temporary disability, it is an economical alternative to a conservatorship.

If you have a living trust, it is important that you also execute a power of attorney. It can be used to transfer assets you might have overlooked into the trust if you become unable to do so. And if your trust allows, it can be used to amend your trust after your incompetency if necessary, for example, to take advantage of the latest tax reform act.

You can even give your spouse the right to make annual exclusion gifts on your behalf to your children and grandchildren long after you no longer have legal capacity to do so yourself.

Community Property Affidavit

If you live in a community property state, this simple document (Appendix K) can pay huge dividends. It converts assets held in joint tenancy to community property. In Chapter 25 we will discuss the advantages of holding property that has gone up in value as community property. For you westerners, this is one of the most important things you will learn in this book!

Nomination of Conservator

As we will see in Chapter 33, a conservatorship is a judicial proceeding in which the court appoints an individual or an institution to handle your affairs if you are unable to do so yourself. Did you know you can nominate your own conservator even if you may never need a conservatorship? You can nominate a conservator in your Durable Power of Attorney for Health Care or in a separate Nomination of Conservator (Appendix L).

In most conservatorships the conservator must post a bond. The bond protects the conservatorship from loss if the conservator takes a powder to Monaco with the conservatorship assets. Bonds can be expensive. Therefore, when your nominee is a trusted relative or a close family friend, you may wish to waive the bond requirement in your nomination.

In the next chapter we will treat a subject that most of us would just as soon avoid—planning for our untimely death.

PROVIDING FOR YOUR ORPHANS

$\mathcal{S}$mall wonder we procrastinate when it comes to planning our estates. To plan an estate is to concede to our mortality; it is to hear at our back "time's winged chariot hurrying near."

Worse yet, to plan well we must advert to unpleasant eventualities, such as an untimely death, that may leave young children orphaned. Plan we must, however, for the consequences of not doing so can be unfortunate.

Guardianship of the Person

As long as either you or your spouse is living, the surviving spouse will most likely provide for the needs of any minor children. On the death of the surviving spouse, however, or if both you and your spouse die in a common disaster, the court will appoint a guardian of the person of your minor children. This guardian will have the responsibility of raising your children. In your will you should designate the person or persons you want to assume this task. Remember, if you appoint a married couple as guardians, you should state what is to happen if the couple's marriage collapses. And you should discuss the guardianship with the persons you name to make sure they are willing to accept the responsibility.

Guardianship of the Estate

If you leave property outright to minor children by will (or living trust), joint tenancy, or life insurance, the court will appoint a guardian of your children's estate who will have the responsibility of managing your children's property until they reach the age of majority.

You can designate this person in your will. Estate guardianships, however, have disadvantages. For example, a guardianship bond will be required, which can be expensive. Also, the guardian must file periodic accountings and obtain court approval before making certain sales, investments, or distributions, which can add to the cost.

Most importantly, the estate must be distributed to your child at his or her majority. And if your child dies before reaching majority, the estate will be distributed to the child's heirs. This may not be what you want.

Gifts in Trust

Is there an alternative to a guardianship of the estate? Yes. In your will or your living trust, you can set up a trust for your children. A trust has two major advantages.

First, you have great flexibility in just how you want the trust administered and distributed. For example, you can establish a separate trust for each child that makes staggered distributions. One-half of the trust could be distributed to your child when he or she reaches 25 and the balance at age 30. Or you can provide for a single trust (known as a family pot trust) to be held for the benefit of all your children until the youngest child reaches 21 or whichever age you designate.

Second, if a child dies before the trust terminates, you can direct to whom distribution of the child's share should be made—to the child's spouse, for example, or the child's children, or your other children.

Gift to a Custodian

This simple alternative to a trust can also avoid the necessity of a guardianship. You can make a gift in your will to a custodian for your child under the Uniform Transfers to Minors Act. The custodian you appoint can manage your child's estate and pay your child's expenses without any court supervision. This means no bonds, no accountings, and probably no attorneys' fees. And, in most states, you can delay the distribution of the custodial account to your child until age 25.

Special Needs Trust

If you have a disabled child who is receiving or is likely to receive public benefit assistance, there is an added concern. A bequest to a child may disqualify the child from receiving that assistance. You should consider leaving the child's bequest to a special needs trust. In this trust the trustee's authority is limited to providing your child with only those benefits not paid for by public assistance.

The two most common forms of public assistance are Supplemental Security Income (SSI) and Medicaid. SSI provides cash for food, clothing, and shelter to disabled, blind, or aged (65 or older) individuals. Medicaid pays for medical and nursing home care. Both SSI and Medicaid are need based. In other words, to be eligible, an individual must have no more than a specified amount of income and assets. Remarkably, in determining eligibility neither the applicant's personal residence nor his or her car (if necessary for employment or medical treatment), regardless of value, is counted. Nor are assets held in a special needs trust, provided the beneficiary does not have the power to revoke the trust nor to direct the use of the trust assets for his or her own support.

Special needs trusts can provide a beneficiary with significant benefits not provided by public assistance such as dental care, special therapy, eyeglasses, computer equipment, and even vacations and entertainment. However, it does not give the beneficiary the independence of outright ownership. Therefore, you should analyze the desirability of a special needs trust in light of the following considerations:

- The amount of money available to fund the special needs trust.
- The value of the public benefits that may be available to your child.
- Other sources of medical benefits (i.e., existing medical insurance) available to your child.
- Whether your child's disability is progressive.
- Whether your child is institutionalized or likely to be institutionalized.
- And most importantly, the desires of your child. If your child is living independently, ask him or her what is more important, qualification for public assistance or the freedom of outright ownership.

In the next chapter you will learn why cowboys pay fewer taxes.

ONE MORE REASON TO HEAD OUT WEST

*I*f you live in a community property state (namely, Arizona, California, Idaho, Louisiana, Nevada, New Mexico, Texas, Washington, or Wisconsin), the way in which you and your spouse hold title to property has significant income tax consequences. In fact, Uncle Sam, in a rare outburst of generosity, has made tax savings available in community property states that are not available elsewhere. To illustrate how this beneficence can save you taxes, we will turn again to the Artful Dodger, who, as we know, has raised tax avoidance to an "art" form.

Capital Gains Tax

You will recall that years ago Art had the foresight to buy 100 shares of Black, Inc. for $100, which has soared in value to $10,000. (If you don't, I'm sure Art will be happy to regale you with the details.) If Art sells the stock, he will pay income tax on the difference between the original cost of $100 (known as his tax basis) and the sales price of $10,000.

If Art dies owning these shares of Black, Inc., however, his original tax basis is "stepped up" to the stock's value (say $10,000) at his death. If Ellie sells Black, Inc. for $10,000 after Art's death, no income tax is payable. If Ellie dies before Art, since Ellie didn't own Black, Inc., Art's basis is unaffected and remains at $100.

If, instead, Art and Ellie own Black, Inc. as joint tenants, upon either's death, the basis will be stepped up but only to one-half the difference between the cost basis of $100 and the value at death of $10,000. The new basis will be $5,050 ($100 plus $4,950). If the surviving spouse sells the stock for $10,000, the remaining $4,850 is taxed.

When Art and Ellie told their Clever Attorney they owned Black,

Inc. (along with their residence and other appreciated assets) in joint tenancy, the Clever Attorney wouldn't let them out the door until they had signed a Community Property Affidavit (Appendix K) stating that all these joint tenancy assets were really community property. As a result, the situation will be dramatically different on the death of the first spouse. The basis of the stock, as if it had been sprinkled with pixie dust, will be stepped up to $10,000 regardless of whether Art or Ellie is the first to die. If the surviving spouse sells the stock for $10,000, no income tax is payable.

Holding title as community property has one other advantage. On Art's death, for example, since community property assets get a stepped-up tax basis, Ellie will not have to go rooting through Art's business records (located in a cardboard box, God knows where) to try to figure out the original cost of each asset.

How to Save It

Here are some ways you can take advantage of these rules and save income taxes.

> Do you and your spouse own a residence? If so, pull out the deed to your residence. Chances are you and your spouse hold title as joint tenants. (This is probably because the person at the title company told you to take title this way.) If your residence has gone up in value, convert it to community property along with any other appreciated joint tenancy property. This may be as simple as executing a Community Property Affidavit (Appendix K). This way the surviving spouse will get a full step up in basis on the death of the other spouse. Be careful, however. If you own joint tenancy assets that have gone down in value, you may not want to change them to community property. A joint tenancy asset that has depreciated gives the surviving spouse a bigger income tax loss than in the case of an asset held as community property. In this case, it is better not to execute an all-inclusive Community Property Affidavit but, instead, to transfer to community property only those assets that have appreciated.

✒ Do you and your spouse each own appreciated separate property? If so, each of you should transfer separate property of
equal value to community property. Then no matter which of
you dies first, the survivor will get a full step up in basis on all
the converted property.

✒ What if you own appreciated separate property but your
spouse doesn't? Consider transferring it to community property
even if your spouse cannot match the transfer with separate
property of his or her own. If your spouse dies before you, you
will get a step up in the tax basis on the community property
that was formerly your separate property. Obviously, this
strategy raises considerations that go beyond tax planning. You
will be making a transfer of your separate property to community property that once made is irrevocable. If you and your
spouse divorce, you will doubtless come to regard this bit of tax
planning as unenlightened.

But hold on! All of this may change in 2010. Because if Uncle Sam
sticks to his guns and abolishes estate taxes altogether, he will limit the
step up in basis to $1,300,000 ($4,300,000 for transfers to a spouse).
Since 2010 is a long way off, let's not worry about the details just yet.

For those of you wondering whether to squeeze in one last chapter
before bedtime, the answer is "don't," because the next chapter and the
two following are among the toughest in this book, so much so they
send even the Clever Attorney to the medicine cabinet.

IRA STANDS FOR IMPOSSIBLE
TO READILY APPREHEND

Author's note: Prior to 2001, the rules applying to IRAs had become so complex that even Uncle Sam didn't understand them. So in January of that year Uncle Sam proudly announced new IRA rules he promised would make life simpler for most of us. And they do. Except, as you will see, they're still no stroll in the park. The rules for other types of retirement plans such as pension plans, profit sharing plans, and the like, are similar to those governing IRAs, but they are not identical.

One hot afternoon Carol, the Clever Attorney's secretary, announced, "Art just dropped by to discuss his IRA." "Send him in," the Clever Attorney sighed as his hand involuntarily groped in his lower desk drawer for the ibuprofen. It was not so much that he minded Art's habit of dropping in unannounced, which he did; it was that Uncle Sam, even with his much-heralded reform, has created a set of rules so complex they would be the envy of a Byzantine emperor. And explaining them to Art in the Clever Attorney's Swedish sauna of an office would be no joy.

Almost since Art was in knickers, he has made yearly tax-free contributions to his IRA account. Since this money has been compounding tax-free, Art has managed to tuck away more than $1,000,000. Art understands Uncle Sam will tax every penny he withdraws from his IRA at ordinary income tax rates so he wants to delay taking the money out of his IRA for as long as possible. "When do I have to take the money out of my IRA?" Art wants to know.

Not Too Soon and Not Too Late

Under normal circumstances, Art cannot take money out of his IRA before he is 59^1/$_2$ without incurring a 10% tax in addition to ordinary income taxes on any premature distributions. Art must begin taking the money out when he reaches 70^1/$_2$. If he doesn't, Uncle Sam will exact a penalty equal to 50% of the money Art should have taken out but didn't.

Not Too Much and Not Too Little

It used to be that if Art took too much out of his IRA, he had to pay a 15% excise tax on the excess distributions. But no more. Now all Art has to worry about is taking too little. For if he takes too little, Uncle Sam will slap him with that same 50% penalty on the money he should have taken out.

Let Me Count the Ways

At retirement, Art has a number of options:

1. Art could withdraw all his IRA in a lump sum. This is not the way to reduce income taxes because, problem is, the whole IRA is subject to income tax all at once. "Is there any way I can take out less?" asks Art. Yes . . .

2. To allow Art to take out less, Uncle Sam invented a hypothetical person who is exactly ten years younger than Art. Think of this hypothetical person as the person you would like to see staring back at you in the bathroom mirror each morning. In Art's case, he has less of a paunch, more hair, and, most importantly, a longer life expectancy. This is important since Uncle Sam allows Art to take money out of his IRA over a number of years based on the joint life expectancy of Art and this hypothetical person. For example, at age 70, this joint life expectancy is 27.4 years and Art must withdraw $36,496 in the first year of his retirement ($1,000,000 divided by 27.4).

"But I plan to live to be 100," says Art. "Does this mean that my IRA will run out of money by the time I'm 97.4 years old?" No, because each year this joint life expectancy is recalculated upward. By the time Art is

80, he and his 70-year-old counterpart have a joint life expectancy of 18.7 years and withdrawals are based on the assumption that Art will live to be 98.7 (in insurance jargon Art is "chasing his actuarial tail"). As a result of annual recalculation, Art can spread his IRA withdrawals over an increasingly greater life expectancy, so no matter how long he lives, his well will never run dry. Even if Art lives to be 115 or older, the most he has to withdraw in any year from then on is just over one-half.

(There is one situation in which everything the Clever Attorney just told Art is wrong. For if Ellie were more than ten years younger than Art, distributions would be calculated over the joint life expectancy of Art and his much younger wife rather than that of Art and the hypothetical person.)

"That's O.K., so far as it goes, but what happens when I die if Ellie survives me?" asks Art. The Clever Attorney takes a deep breath (at which point he is wondering when the ibuprofen will kick in):

Though there are other options available to Ellie, she will probably choose to "roll over" Art's IRA into her IRA and thus, make it her own. Only surviving spouses have this option. Ellie gets a fresh start and, just like Art, her withdrawals are based on the joint life expectancy of herself and that same eternally younger person. Since it's now her IRA, Ellie can name her own beneficiary and she doesn't have to start making withdrawals until she is 70½.

"What happens on Ellie's death?"

Unlike Ellie, Roger (the beneficiary Ellie named) does not have the right to roll over the IRA and make it his own. Nor can he take advantage of that hypothetical younger chap to spread out his withdrawals. He must make withdrawals over his life expectancy determined in the year after Ellie's death, and he doesn't get to recalculate annually. So if Roger is 45 at Ellie's death, he has a 38.8-year life expectancy. If Roger lives to be 84, he will have drawn the IRA down to zero.

"What if Ellie dies before I do?" Art asks.

Distributions to Art are unaffected by Ellie's death. At Art's death, Roger, the beneficiary Art named after Ellie, must make withdrawals over his life expectancy determined in the year after Art's death.

"Solely out of curiosity, what if I were to name a charity as beneficiary?" Art asks.

Some of you readers may be under the foolish impression that a dead person has no life expectancy. Not in IRA land, for if Art names a charity, minimum distributions will be calculated over Art's life expectancy in the year of his death. This is O.K., for the charity doesn't pay income taxes anyway. But if Art names his estate as beneficiary (or fails to name a beneficiary, in which case his estate will be the beneficiary), the same result applies and the beneficiaries of Art's estate are stuck with taking distributions over Art's life expectancy. If Art dies before attaining age 70^1/$_2$, however, the IRA must be distributed over five years.

Since this stuff is pretty technical, not to mention tedious, I'm going to give you a break here. When you feel up to it, we will take up where we left off in the next chapter; but I warn you, it doesn't get to be just lots more fun.

IRA STANDS FOR IMPOSSIBLE TO READILY APPREHEND— CONTINUED

When we left off last time, the Clever Attorney had just explained how distributions of Art's IRA would be made to Art during his life and to Art's family members at his death. Art, who to the exasperation of the Clever Attorney is showing not the slightest signs of fatigue, persists.

Naming a Trust as Beneficiary

"Can I provide for Ellie in my IRA but also make sure that what's left over will go to Roger?" asks Art. By now Art has nearly worn out the Clever Attorney's patience (as well as his Right Guard). But the Clever Attorney perseveres.

Yes. As the dutiful reader will recall, Art has set up a QTIP trust (see Chapter 3) for the benefit of Ellie during her lifetime. If certain technical requirements are met (which for once in the history of tax planning are not that difficult), Art can name his QTIP trust as beneficiary of his IRA and even though a trust does not have a life expectancy, Uncle Sam allows Ellie to "look through" the trust and take minimum distributions with reference to her life expectancy. At Art's death, therefore, the QTIP trustee must withdraw from the IRA each year an amount determined on the basis of Ellie's life expectancy or the income generated by the IRA, whichever is greater. The trustee must then turn around and distribute to Ellie, at a minimum, the income earned by the IRA, and Ellie must have the right to insist that all assets of the IRA generate reasonable income. At Ellie's death, since Art has named Roger as the next beneficiary of the QTIP trust, what's left in the IRA must be distributed to Roger over Ellie's remaining life expectancy. Since Roger didn't own the IRA, there is no penalty for distributions to him before he reaches age 59^1/$_2$.

Art can also name his bypass trust (see Chapter 4) as beneficiary. This is useful if Art lacks enough other assets to fill up the bypass trust to the amount of his estate tax exemption. On Art's death, the bypass trustee must withdraw from the IRA each year an amount determined on the basis of Ellie's life expectancy, but unlike the QTIP trust, the trustee need not withdraw income generated by the IRA, if greater than the IRA distributions. The trustee can pay to Ellie whatever is necessary for her support, and at Ellie's death what's left in the IRA is distributable to Roger over Ellie's remaining life expectancy, free of estate taxes. (As is always the case, however, Roger must still pay income taxes on IRA withdrawals.)

Finally, if Ellie doesn't need Art's IRA for her support, Art can name his generation-skipping trust (see Chapter 7) as beneficiary. At Art's death, the trustee of the generation-skipping trust (probably Roger) must withdraw from the IRA amounts based on the shortest life expectancy of all trust beneficiaries (in this case, Roger). In addition, the trustee can then pay to Roger from the trust whatever is necessary for Roger's support. At Roger's death, what is left in the generation-skipping trust will pass to the little Dodgers free of tax in Roger's estate. Art must make sure his IRA contains no more than $1,500,000 (or the applicable estate tax exemption amount) at his death, or Uncle Sam will sock his beneficiaries with a confiscatory generation-skipping tax.

One Drawback

One problem with naming a trust as Art's IRA beneficiary is that the trust will pay income taxes on any income not distributed annually. And trusts pay more income taxes than individuals. For example, a trust reaches a 39% tax bracket with income of only $8,000, while Art doesn't reach this bracket until he has earned income of $278,000.

"So what would you do if you were I?" asked Art. The Clever Attorney had finally had enough. "If I were you, I would invite me across the street to Mac's Tea Room to sample some of Mac's Vin Tres Ordinaire," replied the Clever Attorney. And Art did.

THE IRA, PHILOSOPHICALLY SPEAKING

*I*n the cool recesses of Mac's, two glasses of plonk, drained to the lees, gradually restored the Clever Attorney to conviviality, and at Art's urging he began to discuss some broader strategies that apply to Art's retirement planning.

The Name of the Game Is Stretch It Out

Remember, after age 59½ Art can take as much out of his IRA as he likes without penalty. Art's goal, however, should be to stretch out IRA distributions over as many years as possible. (Unless, of course, the Dodgers require more of the IRA for their own needs.) This is because IRAs compound tax-free, and the longer Art can keep his IRA compounding tax-free, the more of it will be available for eventual distribution.

The Double Whammy

All good things, including tax-free compounding, must someday come to an end. Art's IRA is subject to both income tax and estate tax. Even though Art's beneficiary is entitled to deduct the estate taxes paid to Uncle Sam from the IRA income, the effect of the two taxes can be devastating. For example, let's assume Art names Roger as the beneficiary of his million-dollar IRA, and that at Art's death, Roger, who cannot wait to get his hands on the money, withdraws the whole thing. After paying estate and income taxes out of the IRA, Roger could end up with as little as $268,537.

Let's look at some strategies to help Art avoid this unhappy result.

The Spousal Rollover

Naming Ellie as Art's beneficiary works great if Ellie survives Art. For Ellie can roll over Art's IRA and name a new beneficiary such as Roger or, better yet for stretching our purposes, the little Dodgers, thus extending distributions out over several generations.

Wait and See

No one, not even Art, knows what the future may bring. Art is, therefore, in a dither over whether he should name Ellie, his bypass trust, or Roger as the beneficiary of his IRA. Art can "copper his bets" by naming Ellie as his first beneficiary, the bypass trust as his second beneficiary, and Roger as his third beneficiary. If, at Art's death, there are not enough assets to fill up the bypass trust, Ellie can disclaim whatever portion of the IRA is necessary to top it off. Or if she doesn't need the IRA, Ellie, as beneficiary of the bypass trust, can disclaim the IRA. In this way, Roger will become the beneficiary of the IRA just as if Art had named him in the first place.

Paying Estate Taxes out of Non-IRA Assets

On Art's death if estate taxes can be paid out of non-IRA assets, the entire IRA can continue to compound free of income taxes. Although not always economically feasible, life insurance can sometimes provide the cash necessary to pay estate taxes so the IRA can be kept intact.

Breaking Up Is Not So Hard to Do

If Art names a QTIP trust as beneficiary, Roger must wait for Ellie's death before he receives the first nickel. What if, instead, Art names Ellie and Roger as equal beneficiaries of his IRA? Whose life expectancy will control how the IRA is distributed? If Ellie and Roger split the IRA account into two accounts of equal value on or before September 30th of the year following Art's death, Ellie can roll her half of Art's IRA over into her own IRA and Roger can begin receiving distributions that will be stretched out over his life expectancy. Splitting an IRA between a spouse and children is an attractive alternative to leaving the IRA to a QTIP trust especially when the IRA owner's spouse is not the parent of the IRA owner's children.

Splitting IRAs can also get rid of beneficiaries with no life expectancies. Let me explain. If Ellie left her IRA to Roger and charity equally, since the charity doesn't have a life expectancy, the IRA must be distributed over Ellie's remaining life expectancy <u>unless</u> the IRA is split, in which case distribution can be made immediately to the charity and Roger can take his half of the IRA out over his life expectancy.

But remember, Uncle Sam doesn't allow IRA splitting when a trust is named as a beneficiary. So if Art names his bypass trust as beneficiary and if Roger and the little Dodgers are the beneficiaries of the bypass trust, distributions must be made over the life of the oldest beneficiary, i.e., Roger.

Gifts to Charity

We know that Art is not charitably disposed, but Ellie is. If Ellie wants to leave something to her favorite charity, why not name the charity as the beneficiary of her IRA? Under the new rules, Ellie gets to stretch out her IRA distributions just as if she had named an individual as beneficiary. At her death, her IRA escapes not only estate tax but also income tax. The charity receives 100% of the IRA, and Uncle Sam not a farthing.

Or if Ellie wants to provide for Roger, she can name a charitable remainder trust (see Chapter 15) as her IRA beneficiary, designating Roger as the lifetime beneficiary of the trust. At Ellie's death Roger receives annual payments from the trust during his lifetime, but at his death the balance passes to charity. Ellie must be careful, however. Only the charitable portion of Ellie's IRA escapes tax at her death, and the IRA, since it passes into a charitable trust, is not available for the payment of the estate taxes on Roger's lifetime interest. Therefore, Ellie must make sure there are sufficient assets in the rest of her estate to pay the balance of the estate tax. (If Ellie had named Art as the beneficiary of the charitable remainder trust, however, there would be no tax at Ellie's death, since the gift qualifies for the marital deduction.)

Or Ellie can name her favorite charity and Roger as equal beneficiaries of her IRA. But be careful! For, it bears repeating that unless the charity's half of the IRA is distributed to it on or before September 30th of the year following Ellie's death, the half passing to Roger will be spread out over Ellie's remaining life expectancy not Roger's.

What's Mine Is Yours

Thus far, we have been referring to Art's IRA or Ellie's IRA as if it were really Art's IRA or Ellie's IRA. Remember, in a community property state, if Art's IRA was earned during marriage, it is community property and Ellie has a half interest in it. So, if Art names a beneficiary other than Ellie, he must get Ellie's consent or risk a nasty lawsuit down the road.

Roth IRA

In 1998 Uncle Sam heard a rumor that a group of Stanford professors, working around the clock in a secret underground library, were actually beginning to understand how IRAs work. "Not on my watch," he declared, and he set about inventing the Roth IRA, which reverses almost all the rules.

For example:

- Art cannot deduct his contributions to the Roth IRA, but
- He can take distributions out tax-free, and
- Art, once he reaches age 59½ (or subsequent beneficiaries, anytime), can withdraw as much or as little of the IRA as he wants without penalty.

If Art's income is below a certain level, he can either contribute annually to a Roth IRA or roll all or part of his existing IRA into a Roth IRA.

The advantage of a Roth IRA is that although Art pays a tax upfront, what is left compounds tax-free and is eventually distributed tax-free at Art's or his beneficiary's choosing. Given enough time to grow, Roth IRAs can produce dramatic income tax savings.

Educational IRA

In 1998 Uncle Sam also invented the educational IRA. For example, Art can contribute up to $2,000 each year to an educational trust for each of the six little Dodgers who is under age 18. Like the Roth IRA, contributions to the educational IRA are not deductible, but distributions for higher education expenses come out tax-free. Art will not pay gift taxes on these contributions, nor will they be subject to estate tax at his death. Also, like the Roth IRA, the educational IRA is limited to individuals with incomes below a certain level.

Do you own life insurance? Maybe you shouldn't. To find out, read on.

LIFE INSURANCE: GET RID OF IT

et's talk about life insurance. Wait! Don't turn the page! I am not trying to sell you anything. There are things you must know about life insurance if you are serious about saving taxes. So read on.

Yes, It's Taxable

Years ago the Artful Dodger purchased a $100,000 policy of life insurance naming his son, Roger, as the beneficiary. Art is the owner of the policy. He is also the insured, since it is his death that will trigger the payoff of $100,000. Roger, as the beneficiary, will get the money.

Art is shocked to discover that on his death the $100,000 will be taxed in his estate. What is especially galling to Art is that he purchased life insurance to pay estate taxes, not to create them. In addition to a couple of Valiums, Art needs some basic tax advice.

The Solution

There is a simple solution to Art's problem: Art should give the insurance policy to Roger. Art will still be the insured and Roger will still be the beneficiary. Only the ownership of the policy will change.

"Do you mean to tell me that insurance on my life can be owned by someone other than me?" Art asks. Absolutely.

"Isn't that a taxable gift?" Art persists. Probably not. Although the proceeds from the policy at Art's death will be $100,000, the policy's value while Art is alive is relatively small. If it is under $11,000, Art can give the policy to Roger tax-free under the annual exclusion. (Remember the annual exclusion?) Together, Art and Ellie can give Roger an insurance policy worth $22,000 tax-free.

Now for the really exciting news! At Art's death, since Art no longer owns the life insurance the $100,000 will pass to Roger tax-free, that is, free of estate tax and free of income tax.

But Be Careful

"So what's the hitch?" asks Art, who has been on guard ever since he lost his shirt in a tax shelter having something to do with recycling used dental floss. Only two hitches: First, Art must survive the gift by three years or the entire $100,000 will be taxed in his estate. Second, Roger, not Art, should pay future insurance premiums or some of the $100,000 will be taxed in Art's estate. (Art, however, can give Roger the money to pay the premiums.)

A Better Solution

Art can go one step further. He can name Roger's children as beneficiaries and then give the policy to the children. In this way he can transfer $100,000 to his grandchildren tax-free. The $100,000 is thus taxed in neither Art's nor Roger's estate. This may present a problem if there is a chance Roger's children will cash in the policy the first time they walk past a store window displaying motorized scooters.

As you know from reading Chapter 9, Art can solve this problem by transferring the policy to the trustee of an irrevocable trust or to a custodian under the Uniform Transfers to Minors Act who will administer the insurance proceeds on Art's death for the benefit of the grandchildren.

In most cases, transferring ownership of insurance policies can be accomplished easily and without the need for a lot of high-priced legal talent. In fact, a call to your insurance agent is usually all it takes to obtain the forms necessary to make the change. And the tax savings can be dramatic!

In the next chapter we are going to travel to some pretty exotic islands. The question is, should we take all our earthly possessions with us?

GO OFFSHORE, YOUNG MAN

*O*ur favorite worrywart, the Artful Dodger, has been losing sleep, not to mention hair, lately. Now that he has scads of money, he is obsessed by the idea that someone, besides Uncle Sam, will try to take it away from him. Art has read about juries awarding great gobbets of cash for injuries not much worse than a hangnail. Lately, in the watch hours of the morning, he's had dark visions of his home being sold at sheriff's auction, of his tanning booth being repossessed.

Art was, therefore, all ears when a golfing buddy boasted that he, along with all of the other "smart money" guys, had "gone offshore" with their assets.

Art immediately rushed off to his Clever Attorney to see if he too could join the ranks of the smart-money guys.

Going Offshore

Indeed, so-called foreign protection of assets trusts have generated much interest lately. So much so that a latter-day Horace Greeley might be heard to say, "Go offshore, young man, go offshore." For which one of us isn't beguiled by the dream of sitting on a beach next to a stack of hard-earned dollars, watching our creditors pile up on the reef? Unfortunately, as Art learned, for most of us the dream may have a morning-after.

The idea of an offshore trust is simple. The grantor creates a trust under the laws of a foreign country and then transfers his or her assets into the trust. The trust makes distributions to family members such as his or her spouse and their children. At the end of the term of the trust, the grantor can either take the assets back or, if creditors are still lurking, extend the trust.

Fraudulent Conveyances

The trust does not save taxes. Its sole objective is to protect assets from creditors. But creditors have protections, too.

For example, a transfer to an offshore trust cannot be a fraudulent conveyance. In 1571, the Statute of Elizabeth declared void all transfers of property made with the intent of defrauding creditors. The United States and many other countries have similar statutes. The offshore trust must be established under the laws of a foreign country that recognizes trusts but that isn't overly bothered by the Statute of Elizabeth. Currently some of these countries are the Bahamas, the Cayman Islands, the Cook Islands, Cyprus, and Gibraltar.

Nonetheless, the grantor should also be concerned with the fraudulent conveyance laws here at home. Some grantors smugly assume that any U.S. judgment against them based on a fraudulent conveyance will be unenforceable in the foreign country of their trust. This may be, but assets such as the family residence remaining in the United States are still subject to creditors' claims. Moreover, the grantor might be subject to criminal penalties.

Offshore trusts also create problems for the attorney. For whom do you think the creditors will chase when they discover that the grantor's assets have all gone on an island vacation? Perhaps the solution is that no attorney should draft an offshore trust who doesn't have one of his or her own.

Offshore trusts tend to be expensive. They can cost more than $15,000 to set up and $5,000 or more per year thereafter to maintain.

On balance, offshore trusts raise significant legal, financial, and ethical questions. For a few the offshore trust may be a panacea; but for the rest of us it will remain a dream.

The Alaskan Trust

A few years ago a bunch of Clever Alaskan Attorneys were tossing a few back with some members of the Fairbanks chamber of commerce. The chamber folks were complaining about the difficulty of attracting tourists to Alaska during the winter season, which runs roughly from August 15 to July 15. The Alaskan attorneys were complaining about the really Clever Attorneys in the Bahamas, the Cayman Islands, the

Cook Islands, Cyprus, and Gibraltar who were making satchels of money from offshore trusts. Somebody, no one can remember who, said something about opportunity being the twin sister of adversity, and before you could say "aurora borealis," the Alaskan trust was born.

The Alaskan trust

1. Is irrevocable,
2. Allows distributions to be made to you,
3. Can last as long as you want, but
4. Most importantly, unlike the offshore trusts, it is free from the claims of creditors that arise only *after* you set it up.

Of course, you must hire one of those Clever Alaskan Attorneys to draft the trust and an Alaskan trust company to manage it, which is not cheap. Since the invention of the Alaskan trust, other states that also have severe winters, such as Delaware, Idaho, Illinois, South Dakota, and Wisconsin, are rushing to copy Alaska's "creditor proof" trusts.

Next we will look at some less exotic, more traditional ways of keeping creditors at bay.

31

PROTECTING YOUR BOOTY

When we last saw the Artful Dodger, he was in a state of acute paranoia over the prospect of hordes of creditors swooping down to plunder his precious possessions. (This is highly unlikely since Art is the type of person who rushes down to pay his monthly utility bill in person and has receipts to prove it going back to the Truman administration.) Having reluctantly decided to pass on the offshore trust and the Alaskan trust, Art is casting about for more conventional ways to preserve wealth. So he dropped by his Clever Attorney's office to have a chat.

Exempt Assets

First off, under state law even the most rapacious creditor cannot grab certain assets. The states have widely varying exemption laws. For example, in California, Art, having reached the age of 65, finds that he and Ellie have a homestead exemption of $100,000. This means that up to $100,000 of equity in the family residence is secure. (Art's son, Roger, and his wife, because neither is 65, have an exemption of $75,000.) If the Dodgers lived in Texas, they would have an unlimited homestead exemption. But if they lived in New York, their homestead exemption would be a paltry $10,000.

Most states also exempt automobiles, household furnishings and personal effects, jewelry and works of art, life insurance policies, and certain retirement benefits. However, most of these exemptions are limited to a modest value.

Although state exemptions are nice to have around, they are so limited that they provide little comfort to most of us.

Living Trusts

Forget living trusts as a means of protecting assets. At best, a living trust may slow but will not stop the onslaught of creditors.

Tax-Saving Trusts

Perhaps you recall the various tax-saving trusts Art can set up for Ellie: the bypass trust that escapes tax in Ellie's estate, and the QTIP trust that qualifies for the marital deduction (or the qualified domestic trust, if the surviving spouse is not a U.S. citizen).

Each of these trusts, if properly drafted, contains a spendthrift provision. This provision states that the trust is exempt from the claims of the beneficiary's creditors. Thus, on Art's death, assets placed in these trusts will be securely tucked away for Ellie's benefit. Creditors can only look longingly at these trust assets, much as Aesop's fox looked at the hanging grapes.

Charitable Trusts

In Chapter 15 we discussed the tax advantages of Art's creating a charitable remainder trust. A charitable remainder trust also gives Art protection against creditors during his and Ellie's lifetime. True, the assets in the trust cannot be touched. Art's creditors can, however, reach trust distributions after Art has received them. If Art dislikes the idea of creditors swooping down on these distributions, he can draft a charitable remainder trust in such a way that it pays him the stated percentage (e.g., 5%) or trust income, whichever is less. He can instruct the trustee to invest solely in growth stock. Then there will be no distributions upon which to swoop. And Art can delay receiving trust distributions until his financial troubles have blown over.

All of this makes Art feel somewhat more secure. But at night, on his headboard, the black crows of worry still roost. Perhaps in the next chapter we can put a few of these birds to flight.

PROTECTING MORE OF YOUR BOOTY

Recently, the Artful Dodger's spirits have been on the rise. He now knows creditors can't reach the money he will receive from his charitable trust. Moreover, at his death the property he leaves in trust to his wife, Ellie, also will be protected. To the annoyance of everyone around him, Art has taken to singing, under his breath, over and over again, "Oh, no, they can't take that away from me." Eager to learn more about asset protection, Art wandered back into his Clever Attorney's office to find out more about protecting his booty.

Generation-Skipping Trusts

In estate planning, Art can do for his son, Roger, what Art cannot do for himself. For example, Art cannot protect his property from his creditors' claims merely by creating a living trust. Art can, however, give Roger property in trust either during Art's life or at death. If the trust contains a spendthrift clause, the property will be outside the reach of Roger's creditors. Moreover this trust can continue on for the benefit of the little Dodgers after Roger's death.

As we discussed in Chapter 5, the primary purpose of such a trust is to pass Art's property to his grandchildren (Roger's children) without its being taxed in Roger's estate. That the property can pass free of creditors' claims as well is an added bonus.

Art must bear in mind that once the assets of a trust are distributed to a beneficiary, they are no longer protected. Art may decide, therefore, to put a "sprinkling power" in his trust. This allows the trustee to choose to which of Art's family members to make distributions. Thus, the trustee can choose not to make distributions to a child or grand-child whose creditors are camped out on the welcome mat.

Gifts to Spouse

Years ago Art, quite foolishly, became a general partner with his son, Roger, in one of Roger's ill-begotten plans to get rich quick. Although nothing bad has happened yet, Art feels it is only a matter of time before Roger's idiot scheme puts him at personal risk. Art has heard of people, especially professionals, giving their property to a spouse to avoid the claims of potential creditors.

Does this scheme work? Possibly. As we have seen, Art can give Ellie any amount, tax-free. But the gift must not be a fraud on creditors. Also the gift must be irrevocable and cannot be a mere sham. In other words, no crossed-fingers-behind-the-back stuff.

There is one obvious problem. If Ellie ever gets really fed up with Art (and who could blame her?) and divorces him, she gets to keep all the property. And all Art will end up with is Medicaid eligibility.

Transfers of life insurance involve less risk to Art. He can transfer the ownership of life insurance, naming Ellie as the beneficiary, to her, thereby placing both the policy and its proceeds beyond the reach of his creditors. If Art and Ellie do part company, all Art will have lost is the cash surrender value of the policy.

Corporations and Partnerships

Always eager to make more money, Art, in his spare time, has invented a fully biodegradable beer can. Art worries about the liability he might incur if his invention doesn't work out just right. (Several cans, for example, have biodegraded prematurely, leaving a mess in Ellie's refrigerator.)

By incorporating his venture Art can probably limit his liability to the assets of the corporation. A corporation can be fairly simple. In fact, Art may be able to act as sole shareholder, director, and officer.

An alternative to a corporation is the limited liability company (LLC), which is available in many states. The LLC is taxed like a part-nership (which is simpler than a corporation), yet it affords the same protection from liability as a corporation.

Insuring Against the Risk

Many of the most serious risks Art faces, such as those involving personal injury or property damage, are covered by insurance Art has purchased on his home, car, and business. Of course, Art should periodically review these policies to make sure he is adequately protected. He should also consider buying an umbrella policy, which increases the protection afforded by all these policies. Since an umbrella policy only supplements existing insurance, it is surprisingly affordable.

In the next chapter we will explore the question, "Do you need a conservatorship?" Hint: If you think you do, you probably don't.

IF YOU THINK YOU DO, YOU PROBABLY DON'T

*O*ne day the Artful Dodger and his wife, Ellie, dropped in on their Clever Attorney to discuss estate planning. While Art was out wiping the chalk mark off the tire of his Geo Metro, Ellie told the Clever Attorney about something that had been bothering her. At least once a day, Ellie confided, she walks into a room to get something and ends up standing in the middle of the room without any idea why she is there. "Perhaps I should know something about conservatorships," Ellie said, smiling weakly.

Two thoughts popped into the Clever Attorney's head. The first thought he disclosed to Ellie. It was that people who think they may need a conservatorship generally don't; and people who don't often do.

The second thought he kept to himself. It was that he had the same problem as Ellie. Only it happened to him several times each day.

Even though not a candidate for a conservatorship, Ellie wanted to know more about it.

Some Definitions

A conservatorship is a court proceeding to take care of people who cannot take care of themselves or who might fall prey to the undue influence of others. A person does not have to be incompetent to have a conservatorship. In fact, a person who is competent can petition for the appointment of a conservator for himself or herself.

First, let's get the nomenclature out of the way. The person under a disability is the conservatee. The person charged with the responsibility of caring for the conservatee is the conservator. (As you Gilbert and Sullivan fans know, in the case of a minor the parties are known as the ward and the guardian, respectively.)

The conservator of the estate manages the conservatee's property. The conservator of the person manages the conservatee's personal care. This can be the same person.

The Procedure

The laws governing conservatorships vary from state to state. Here is a description of how a typical conservatorship works.

The court proceeding is started when a petition for the appointment of a conservator is filed by an interested party. Unless the petition is filed by the proposed conservatee, the proposed conservatee must be served with a citation advising him or her of the petition and the hearing date and ordering him or her to attend.

Our judicial system zealously protects the rights of incapacitated people, so much so that some jurisdictions employ their own investigators who independently apprise the judge of a conservatee's situation. After the petition is filed, the court investigator interviews the proposed conservatee and files a comprehensive report describing the conservatee's condition. The investigator asks the conservatee if he or she wants the conservatorship and if he or she approves of the proposed conservator. The investigator also makes recommendations as to the need for the conservatorship and the appropriate level of care.

Unless unwilling or physically unable, the proposed conservatee attends the hearing. The judge may question the proposed conservator and conservatee to ensure the appointment is appropriate. If the proposed conservatee objects to being conserved, the court appoints an attorney to represent his or her interests and sets the matter for further hearing at which time the need for a conservatorship will be determined. If the proposed conservatee makes no objection and the court finds it is in his or her best interests, a conservator is appointed and letters of conservatorship issue. These letters give the conservator authority to act on the conservatee's behalf.

In the next chapter we will see how conservatorships can be used to do some crucial estate planning for individuals who, due to their incapacity, cannot do it themselves.

DOING FOR OTHERS . . .

hen we wound up the last chapter, the conservator had just been appointed and letters of conservatorship had been issued.

The Bond

Unless the conservatee is competent and waives it, the court will require the conservator to post a bond. In some states, for example, the amount of the bond is equal to the value of the personal property of the estate plus the estimated annual income earned by those assets. For example, if the conservatorship assets (exclusive of real property) total $500,000, the bond will be set at $525,000, assuming an annual income of 5%. The cost of this bond can range from $600 to $1,200 or more per year.

Think of a bond as an insurance policy that protects the conservatorship estate from loss if the conservator goes "over the hill" with the conservatorship assets. The amount of the bond sometimes can be reduced to the extent assets are deposited in a blocked bank account and receipts are filed with the court.

The Inventory and Appraisal

The conscientious reader of this book will no doubt have noticed the similarity between conservatorship and probate proceedings. (The rest of you really should pay closer attention.) As in the case of probate, the conservator files an inventory with the court, listing all conservatorship assets. These assets are appraised by a court-appointed referee.

Court Reports

Periodically (usually every year or two), the conservator files with the court a report that must include a balanced accounting.

The conservator is entitled to a fee that the judge must approve. This fee is usually based on the hours spent handling the conservatorship. Judges scrutinize these fees and may reduce the fees requested by the conservator or by the conservator's attorney if they are not substantiated. If the conservator is a family member, he or she often waives any fee.

Some important actions of the conservator, such as selling the conservatee's residence, require advance court approval. Before deciding the matter, the judge may order the court investigator to visit the conservatee and advise the judge of the conservatee's wishes and ability to remain in the residence.

It's Never Too Late

A conservator can even petition the court to do estate planning for the conservatee. By this procedure, the court and the conservator can accomplish some of those things the conservatee probably would want to do.

Take the case of the Artful Dodger's Aunt Dottie, who is mentally incompetent. Aunt Dottie never got around to doing much in the way of estate planning. Now she lacks the capacity to write a will, create a trust, or make gifts. As a result, unless something is done, unnecessary estate taxes and administration expenses will be incurred at her death.

In times past, Aunt Dottie's conservator could do little more than wring his or her hands. Today, however, in most states the conservator can petition the court to do many of the things Aunt Dottie could have done were she competent. For example, Aunt Dottie was in the habit of giving her children annual gifts of $11,000. Aunt Dottie's conservator can seek court approval to continue making the gifts on her behalf, thus reducing the size of her taxable estate. The court can also authorize the conservator to set up a living trust for Aunt Dottie to avoid probate, or to change Aunt Dottie's estate plan to save estate taxes.

As you already know, an alternative to a conservatorship is a living trust, which many find attractive because it usually requires no court involvement. One important limitation of the living trust, however, is that the trustee, unlike the conservator, is not permitted to do estate planning for someone like Aunt Dottie.

In the next chapter you will get an entirely biased view of how to pick your own Clever Attorney.

CHOOSING YOUR OWN CLEVER ATTORNEY

Now that you know something about estate planning, you just might want to find your own Clever Attorney to put some of these concepts to work for you. Here are some thoughts on how you might go about this.

Referrals

There is no better way to choose an attorney than to profit from someone else's experience. Ask around among your friends, your accountant, your banker, your analyst. Chances are, before long the names of one or two attorneys will come up over and over again.

If you have had a good experience with an attorney in the past (I know what you're thinking), the obvious place to start is with him or her. Be sure to ask if estate planning is one of his or her specialties. If not, this attorney probably knows the territory and can refer you to someone local who is well regarded professionally.

Advertising

I must warn you that what follows is an entirely biased opinion on the subject of legal advertising: When it comes to choosing an attorney from the Yellow Pages, my advice is, "Let your fingers take a rest." It is simply not true that the size of an ad is inversely proportional to the competency of the attorney. But neither is it any guarantee that the attorney who placed the ad is well qualified. You should no more pick your attorney on the basis of advertising than you would your family doctor.

At one time attorneys were ethically forbidden to advertise. Now, the floodgates are open, and tasteless, sometimes downright misleading ads abound, not only in the Yellow Pages but throughout the media as well. When an attorney tells you in boldface type how wonderful he or she is, take it with a grain of salt.

The Yellow Pages can serve one useful purpose. At the end of all that advertising, look for an "Attorney Guide" listing lawyers who practice in various fields. For an estate planning attorney, look under "Wills, Trusts, and Estate Planning." This guide at least tells you the attorney's own characterization of his or her area of expertise.

Certification

Some state bar associations certify attorneys who have demonstrated proficiency in certain fields. Probate, Estate Planning, and Trusts is one such field. Taxation is another. To become a specialist, an attorney must pass an examination in his or her chosen specialty and then demonstrate both experience and special training in that field. Although some competent estate planners are not certified, certification is one more factor to weigh in your decision.

Peer Review

A national directory of lawyers (known as the *Martindale-Hubbell Law Directory*) is available at most public libraries. Here you can find out, among other things, where an attorney went to school, when he or she graduated, the type of clientele he or she represents, and the area of his or her practice.

More important, you will see how fellow attorneys rate both an attorney's ethics and competency. An attorney's competency is rated C (good to high), B (high to very high), and A (very high to exemplary). An attorney cannot be rated for competency unless she has also attained a V (very high) ethical rating. In the United States, 43% of the attorneys have a CV or higher rating.

Martindale-Hubbell goes to great lengths to obtain a fair consensus of an attorney's reputation from among his or her peers. As a result, attorneys themselves often rely on these ratings when making referrals. Don't overlook this valuable source of information.

Now that you know how to find your own Clever Attorney, let's see how you can assist in preparing the estate plan that's right for you—and for the right price.

36

PREPARING FOR YOUR OWN CLEVER ATTORNEY

Years ago, Art learned in high school physics that there are certain immutable laws of cause and effect. To his dismay, the same immutable laws apply every time he ventures into his Clever Attorney's office to discuss his estate plan—for the predictable effect of each visit is a bill. Here are some suggestions that will reduce the time (not to mention the bill) you (and Art) would otherwise spend with your attorney developing your estate plan.

The Facts

Most estate planning attorneys have clients fill out a questionnaire listing assets and liabilities. If possible, get a copy of this questionnaire, fill it out, and drop it off at your attorney's office before your first conference.

If your attorney has no such questionnaire, make up your own financial statement. Better yet, if you have your personal finances on a computer, run off a statement of assets and liabilities. Be sure to state exactly how each asset is titled. And remember to list all retirement plans along with life insurance policies.

You should also prepare a list of the names and addresses of members of your immediate family, in addition to those persons you named or intend to name in your will (or trust) as beneficiaries or personal representatives (trustees). In large families it is helpful to diagram your family tree, showing the relationships of your nearest relatives. Remember to list relatives who have died leaving children.

Even if you are not giving a farthing to your relatives, your attorney will need this information. At your death the law requires that your heirs be notified even if you disinherited them. This is not out of a misguided sense of fun but rather to give all interested parties notice of a probate or trust proceeding in case they wish to contest it. (Appendixes M and N are sample Confidential Client Questionnaires, containing financial and family information that you may find useful.)

The Documents

Your attorney will want to review certain documents that are important in preparing your estate plan. Remember to bring copies of the following to your first meeting:

- Deeds to real property. If you can't find a deed, the local title company will obtain a copy, usually at no charge, if you provide the assessor's parcel number.
- Life insurance policies, with all change-of-beneficiary forms.
- Buy–sell, partnership, and other agreements relating to any business you own.
- Beneficiary designation statements for all retirement assets (like IRAs and Keogh plans).
- Your existing estate planning documents.

Boning Up

Estate planning has become very complex. Your attorney must try to explain, in a short time, complicated estate planning concepts that took him several semesters in law school to master. Moreover, the attorney who can communicate in plain English has yet to be born. It is no wonder, therefore, that most clients' eyes start to glaze over three minutes into a discussion of QTIP trusts.

The more you already know about the general concepts of estate planning, the better you will understand what your attorney is trying to tell you. And the less time he or she will spend in explanation. It is well worth your time, therefore, to spend a few hours boning up in advance. This knowledge is not hard to come by.

Every bookstore has a legal section with shelves groaning under the weight of estate planning books written for the nonlawyer. I shamelessly hasten to add that this little book is not a bad place to start. And to reward those of you who have stuck it out this far, I have included crib notes for you (Appendix O), summarizing some of the techniques we have discussed. Feel free to take this checklist with you when you next visit your Clever Attorney.

By following these simple suggestions you will enter your attorney's office with an air of sangfroid, prepared to help him or her prepare the estate plan that is right for you.

In the next chapter we will look at some questions you might just want to discuss with your Clever Attorney.

37 QUESTIONS TO ASK YOUR OWN CLEVER ATTORNEY

Nobody, not even the Artful Dodger's Clever Attorney, is perfect. In fact, just the other day Art's Clever Attorney discovered he had screwed up.

Who Should Pay Estate Taxes?

For years Art's Aunt Agnes has lived in a little cottage Art and Ellie own. Since Agnes is as poor as a church mouse, Art and Ellie have willed the cottage to her so that, if she survives them, she will always have a place to live. The Dodgers' wills did not state on whom the burden of estate taxes would fall. As a result, taxes would be prorated among all beneficiaries, and poor Aunt Agnes would have to sell the cottage to pay her share.

Fortunately, this problem was discovered by the Clever Attorney during a routine review of the Dodgers' estate file. Before his second cup of coffee, he was on the phone to the Dodgers suggesting their wills be changed so the cottage will pass to Agnes free of tax.

The point is simple: Be sure to discuss with your attorney upon which beneficiaries you want the burden of taxes to fall.

Estate planning requires detailed fact gathering. Even the cleverest attorney, on occasion, fails to ask questions, such as this one, that are crucial to an estate plan. Here are some other occasionally overlooked questions you should discuss with your Clever Attorney.

What If My Child Dies First?

Art and Ellie have willed most of their estate to their son, Roger. If Roger dies before they do, their estate passes to Roger's children. The Dodgers' wills read this way because that is the way the standard will in their Clever Attorney's word processor reads. But what of Roger's widow, Thelma? Even though Thelma was never a favorite of the Dodgers, Art and Ellie find the vision of the little Dodgers sitting around the dinner table eating smoked salmon while Thelma eats canned tuna disturbing. Art and Ellie may just want to give some of their estate to Thelma, who, after all, will have the responsibility of raising their grandchildren.

How Should I Dispose of Family Heirlooms?

If Art and Ellie had more than one child, like most folks they would probably leave their family heirlooms, memorabilia, jewelry, and the like to their children equally. This often sows the seeds of future sibling warfare. ("Mother always said I could have Aunt Mildred's milking stool.") It is usually not practical to list heirlooms item by item in your will. Ask your attorney about other ways to distribute these assets. For example, you can tag heirlooms with the children's initials. Or attach a letter with specific instructions to your will or trust. Or, if the kids can't agree, designate just how the property can be divided by lot and designate someone outside the family (who, incidentally, will never forgive you) to preside over the division.

Should I Give My Spouse the Right to Decide Who Will Inherit My Estate?

If Art wills his property to Ellie, in trust, he must state what will happen to the property on Ellie's death. Instead of requiring that his estate pass to Roger, Art can give Ellie the right, during her lifetime, to choose how Art's estate ultimately will be distributed among Roger and the little Dodgers. This is called a limited power of appointment.

If Roger doesn't need any more money, Ellie could leave Art's estate to Roger's children instead. And Ellie could choose which of her grandchildren should inherit. For example, she could leave a healthy amount to the grandchild who is selflessly teaching disabled children and little or nothing to the grandchild who dropped out of school at fourteen to express himself on a Harley–Davidson.

For the finale, I have chosen to reveal the legal equivalent of the secret of the universe when it comes to saving taxes.

38

THE ULTIMATE TAX DODGE

For purely theatrical reasons, I have saved the best part for last. Here now is the Godzilla of all tax loopholes.

Let's say you are a single person with $2,000,000. You want to take a cruise around the world in the hopes of meeting a single person with $4,000,000. Want to know how to charge at least 40% of your trip on Uncle Sam's MasterCard? The answer is simple—take the cruise. Or as the Nike people say, "Just do it."

In Ben Franklin's day, a penny saved was a penny earned. That was before estate taxes. Today it is more accurate to say, a penny saved is a penny taxed.

In all of our labyrinthine tax planning we often overlook the fact that consumption is the ultimate tax dodge. Uncle Sam cannot tax it if it isn't there. The virtues we were taught as children—prudence, moderation, thrift—serve us less well as we get older (at least from the standpoint of estate planning).

You all remember Aesop's fable about the ant and the grasshopper. The ant worked sixteen-hour days gathering food for the winter. The grasshopper danced and drank and regaled all his friends with tasteless lawyer jokes. What Aesop didn't tell you was that when the ant died (probably from stress), Uncle Sam made a killing. But when the grasshopper died (probably from a failed liver), Uncle Sam got nothing.

People are either ants or grasshoppers. If you are reading this chapter, you are an ant. The grasshoppers, having no money to worry about, lost interest in this book a long time ago. The problem with you ants is that you can't stop being ants, even when your storerooms are bursting. But you must try.

And, if you are interested, there is an even more advantageous way to spend your money. Why not consider spending it on charity? A charitable gift gives you a double bonus. Not only does the gift escape taxation in your estate, but you also get to deduct it from your current income. If you are in a 37% income tax bracket (both state and federal) and a 48% estate tax bracket, a gift of $1,000 to your favorite charity will cost you only $328. And when you make a gift to charity during your lifetime, you will get the recognition you deserve, now rather than after you are gone.

So whether your consumption takes the form of doing things that give you pleasure or giving money to charity (which also may give you pleasure), Uncle Sam is picking up some of the tab.

One last thought. It is the shared ambition of most of us to reduce our taxes. But we must not forget that a government's ability to tax is at the very base of its ability to survive.

I admit that Uncle Sam's profligacy with our tax dollars at times suggests the need for a conservatorship. He has, however, given us the type of government that has allowed us to accumulate our booty in the first place. So, in the end, perhaps there are worse things you could do than pay some taxes. The Artful Dodger, or course, doesn't agree with this. But Art, as we know, is an especially tough nut.

This is the last chapter because I have pretty much run out of things to say. (It is simply not true that I ran out in Chapter 12.) I have enjoyed writing this little book. I hope it helps you, with the assistance of your own Clever Attorney, create an estate plan that is just right for you. At least, now at cocktail parties, you can let drop mention of QTIPs, QPRTs, or QDOTs with the nonchalance of someone who really knows.

On behalf of myself and the entire Dodger clan, I thank you for your readership.

APPENDIX A

Pickup Tax States

The following states participate in the pickup tax:

Alabama	Nevada
Alaska	New Mexico
Arizona	North Dakota
Arkansas	Oregon
California	Rhode Island
Colorado	South Carolina
District of Columbia	Texas
Florida	Utah
Georgia	Vermont
Hawaii	Virginia
Idaho	Washington
Illinois	West Virginia
Maine	Wisconsin
Minnesota	Wyoming
Missouri	

APPENDIX B

I. WASTING ART'S EXEMPTION

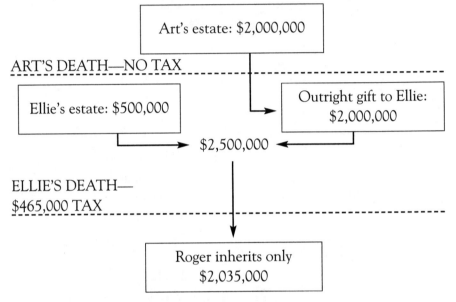

Art's estate: $2,000,000

ART'S DEATH—NO TAX

Ellie's estate: $500,000

Outright gift to Ellie: $2,000,000

$2,500,000

ELLIE'S DEATH—
$465,000 TAX

Roger inherits only $2,035,000

2. GETTING TWO EXEMPTIONS FOR THE PRICE OF ONE

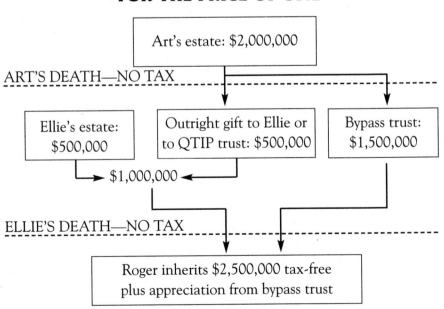

Art's estate: $2,000,000

ART'S DEATH—NO TAX

Ellie's estate: $500,000

Outright gift to Ellie or to QTIP trust: $500,000

Bypass trust: $1,500,000

$1,000,000

ELLIE'S DEATH—NO TAX

Roger inherits $2,500,000 tax-free plus appreciation from bypass trust

APPENDIX C

THE GENERATION-SKIPPING TRUST

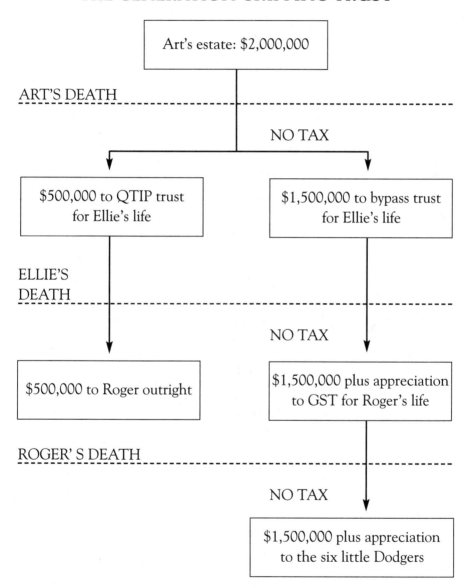

Art's estate: $2,000,000

ART'S DEATH

NO TAX

$500,000 to QTIP trust
for Ellie's life

$1,500,000 to bypass trust
for Ellie's life

ELLIE'S
DEATH

NO TAX

$500,000 to Roger outright

$1,500,000 plus appreciation
to GST for Roger's life

ROGER' S DEATH

NO TAX

$1,500,000 plus appreciation
to the six little Dodgers

APPENDIX D

This form is presented by way of example only.
Do not use this form without the advice of your attorney.

ASSIGNMENT OF TANGIBLE
PERSONAL PROPERTY

The undersigned, _____ and _____,
hereby assign all right, title, and interest in all tangible items of personal
property, all household furniture, furnishings, antiques, art objects, jewelry, precious metals, fine art of every description, and other personal
effects whether now owned or hereinafter acquired, in which either
party has, or both parties have, an interest, to _____
as Trustee of THE _____ TRUST dated _____,
and any amendments made to said trust including those executed after
the date of this assignment.
DATED: _____   _____

                                   [Husband]

                                   _____

                                   [Wife]

APPENDIX E

WILL OF ART DODGER

I, **ART DODGER**, a resident of _____ County, [state], and a citizen of the United States, declare that this is my Will revoking all prior Wills and Codicils.

I

I am married to ELLIE DODGER hereinafter referred to in this Will as my "spouse".

I have one (1) child whose name is ROGER DODGER. I have no deceased children leaving issue.

II

I confirm to my spouse my spouse's interest in our community property. I intend by this Will to control the disposition of all of my separate property, if any, and my one-half (1/2) interest in our community property. I hereby acknowledge that all property owned by my spouse and me as joint tenants, with the exception of cash held in bank accounts, has been transmuted by us to community property.

III

I give my estate to the Trustee of that Trust designated as **The ART AND ELLIE DODGER FAMILY TRUST Dated 200__**, which I have executed today of which I am a Settlor. I direct that my estate be added to, administered, and distributed as part of that trust, according to the terms of the trust, and any amendments made to it before my death. To the extent permitted by law, it is not my intent to create a separate trust by this Will or to subject the trust or the property added to it by this Will to the jurisdiction of the probate court.

If the disposition in this article is not operative or is invalid for any reason, or if the trust referred to in this article fails or has been revoked, then I hereby incorporate by reference the terms of that trust as executed previously without giving effect to any amendments made subsequently, and I bequeath and devise my estate to the Trustee named in the trust as Trustee, to be held, administered, and distributed as provided in the trust instrument.

IV

Except as otherwise provided in this Will, I have intentionally and with full knowledge omitted to provide for my heirs. If any person who, if I died intestate, would be entitled to any part of my estate, and shall either directly or indirectly, alone or in conjunction with any other person, claim in spite of my Will an intestate share of my estate, I give that person One Dollar ($1.00), and no more, in lieu of any other share or interest in my estate.

If any beneficiary under this Will in any manner, directly or indirectly, contests this Will or any of its provisions in any legal proceeding that is designed to thwart my wishes as expressed in this Will, any share or interest in my estate given to that contesting beneficiary under this Will is revoked and shall be disposed of in the same manner provided herein as if that contesting beneficiary had predeceased me without issue.

V

I nominate the persons listed below in the order in which they are named as Executor or successor Executor of my Will:

1. ELLIE DODGER
2. ROGER DODGER

The term "Executor" includes any personal representative of my estate. I request that no bond be required of any Executor nominated in my Will.

My Executor may sell, with or without notice, at either public or private sale, for cash or terms, any property of my estate that my Executor considers necessary for the estate's proper administration and distribution.

My Executor may retain any asset of my estate (including unproductive, speculative, or fluctuating assets) for as long as the Executor considers proper. My Executor shall not be liable for any resulting losses unless the Executor acts in bad faith, is grossly negligent, or engages in willful misconduct.

I authorize my Executor to invest and reinvest any surplus monies in the Executor's hands in any kind of property, real, personal, or mixed, and every kind of investment, specifically including, but not limited to, interest-bearing accounts, corporate obligations of every kind, preferred or common stocks, shares of investment trusts, investment companies, mutual funds, or common trust funds, including funds administered by the Executor and mortgage participations, that people of prudence, discretion, and intelligence acquire for their own account.

I subscribe my name to this Will this ___ day of _____, 200__, at _____, [state].

_____

ART DODGER

On the date written below, **ART DODGER**, testator, declared to us, the undersigned, that this instrument consisting of ___ (_) pages including the page signed by us as witnesses, was the testator's Will and requested us to act as witnesses to it. The testator thereupon signed this Will in our presence, all of us being present at the same time. We now, at the request of the testator and in the presence of the testator and in the presence of each other, subscribe our names as witnesses.

We believe that the testator is over age 18, is of sound mind, and is under no constraint or undue influence.

Executed on _____, 200__, at _____ [state].

We declare under penalty of perjury that the foregoing is true and correct.

_____ residing at _____

_____ residing at _____

APPENDIX F

THE ART AND ELLIE DODGER FAMILY TRUST

THIS TRUST AGREEMENT is entered into and executed on
_____, 2003, by and between ART DODGER and ELLIE
DODGER, of the County of _____, State of [State], herein called
"Settlors", and ART DODGER and ELLIE DODGER, or their Successors, herein called "Trustee".

RECITALS

A. ESTABLISHMENT OF TRUST: The Settlors do hereby execute this trust agreement and as soon as practicable after the establishment of this trust will transfer, assign, and convey to the Trustee by appropriate instruments, and the Trustee shall and does hereby accept, all that certain property described in Schedule A attached hereto and made a part hereof, which, together with any and all other property hereafter conveyed to said Trustee by Settlors or by other persons, including any death benefits made payable to Trustee hereunder, shall constitute and is hereby designated as the "trust estate".

The Trustee shall hold, manage, and distribute the trust estate exclusively for the uses, purposes, and objectives set forth herein, upon and subject to the terms, provisions, and conditions, powers and limitations, set forth herein.

B. FAMILY INFORMATION: Settlors were married on June 19, 1940. Settlors have one (1) child now living whose name is ROGER DODGER by whom they have six (6) grandchildren.

Neither Settlor has any deceased children leaving issue.

ARTICLE I

Section 1.01 Trust Estate.

The trust estate shall be held, administered, and distributed in accordance with this trust agreement. The Settlors declare that any property held by them in joint tenancy prior to its transfer into the trust is, in fact, community property. Any separate property contributed by either Settlor shall retain its character as separate property, any community property transferred to the trust shall remain community property after its transfer. It is the Settlors' intention that the Trustee shall have no more extensive power over any community property transferred to the trust estate than either of the Settlors would have had under California Family Code Sections 1100 and 1102 had this trust not been created, and this trust agreement shall be so interpreted to achieve this intention. This limitation shall terminate on the death of either Settlor.

Section 1.02 <u>Additions to the Trust Estate</u>.

The Settlors, either or both, or any other person desiring to do so for the benefit of any or all of the beneficiaries hereunder, may add property to the trust estate at any time during their respective lives or by testamentary disposition. Such additions shall thereupon come within and be subject to the terms, provisions, conditions, and limitations set forth in this trust agreement.

ARTICLE II

Section 2.01 <u>Community Property During Settlors' Joint Lifetimes</u>.

During the joint lifetimes of the Settlors, the Trustee shall pay to the Settlors for the account of the community, or shall apply for the Settlors' benefit, so much of the net income or principal of the community property held in trust as is necessary in the Trustee's discretion for the Settlors' proper health, education, support, maintenance, comfort, and welfare, in accordance with their accustomed manner of living.

Section 2.02 <u>Separate Property During Settlors' Joint Lifetimes</u>.

During the joint lifetimes of the Settlors, the Trustee shall pay to or apply for the benefit of the Settlor whose separate property was transferred to the trust so much of the net income and principal of that Settlor's separate property as is necessary in the Trustee's discretion for the proper health, education, support, maintenance, comfort, and welfare of that Settlor and the Settlor's spouse in accordance with their accustomed manner of living.

Section 2.03 <u>Revocation During Settlors' Joint Lifetimes and After Death of First Settlor</u>.

During the joint lifetimes of the Settlors, this trust agreement may be revoked in whole or in part with respect to community property by an instrument in writing signed by either Settlor and delivered to the Trustee and the other Settlor, and with respect to separate property, by an instrument in writing signed by the Settlor, who contributed that property to the trust, and delivered to the Trustee. On revocation the Trustee shall promptly deliver to both spouses all or the designated portion of the community property trust assets, which shall continue to be the community property of the Settlors and which shall be held and administered as community property. On revocation with respect to separate property, the Trustee shall promptly deliver to the contributing Settlor all or the designated portion of that separate property.

On the death of the first Settlor, the surviving Settlor shall have the power to amend or revoke the Survivor's Trust only. After the surviving Settlor's death, none of the trusts may be revoked nor their dispositive provisions amended. Revocation and amendment shall be made in the manner provided in this trust instrument.

Section 2.04 <u>Incapacity of Spouse</u>.

If, at any time, either in the Trustee's discretion or as certified in writing by a licensed board-certified physician practicing in the area in which the Settlors reside, either spouse has become physically or mentally incapacitated, whether or not a court of competent jurisdiction has declared him or her to be incompetent, mentally ill, or in need of a conservator, the Trustee shall pay to the other spouse, or apply for the benefit of either Settlor such amounts of net income and principal necessary in the Trustee's discretion for the proper health, support, and maintenance of either or both Settlors in accordance with their accustomed manner of living at the date of this instrument, until the incapacitated Settlor, either in the Trustee's discretion or as certified by a licensed physician, is again able to manage his or her own affairs, or until the earlier death of the incapacitated Settlor. The non-incapacitated spouse may continue to withdraw from time to time accumulated trust income and principal of the community property. Income and principal from community property so paid or withdrawn shall be held and administered as community property by the non-incapacitated spouse. Any income in excess of the amounts applied for the benefit of the Settlors shall be accumulated and added to principal.

Section 2.05 <u>Amendment</u>.

The Settlors may at any time during their joint lifetimes amend the trust agreement or any of its terms by an instrument in writing signed by both Settlors and delivered to the Trustee.

Section 2.06 <u>Powers of Revocation and Amendment Personal to Settlors</u>.

The power of the Settlor[s] to revoke, amend, and withdraw may be exercised only by either or both Settlor[s] personally or by the Conservator of either or both Settlor[s], as the case may be, with court approval or pursuant to authority and for the purposes expressly provided in a durable power of attorney executed by the Settlor[s].

Section 2.07 <u>Powers of Agent Named by Settlors in Durable Powers of Attorney</u>.

Any power of either Settlor of this trust to revoke or amend this trust (including any trust to be established in the future under the provisions of this trust), alone or jointly with the other Settlor, may be exercised by the power-holder's attorney-in-fact, if the document appointing the attorney-in-fact expressly authorizes such action.

In addition, the attorney-in-fact named by either Settlor in a durable power of attorney authorizing such action may withdraw such sums from the Settlor's separate property or interest in the community property for the purpose of making annual exclusion gifts or providing tuition and medical care to those beneficiaries designated in said power of attorney, all so as to qualify for federal gift tax exclusion.

ARTICLE III

Section 3.01 <u>Compensation of Trustee</u>.

The Trustee and any successor Trustee, both corporate and individual, shall be entitled to reasonable compensation for services together with all costs and expenses incurred by such Trustee.

Section 3.02 <u>Resignation of Trustee</u>.

A Trustee may resign by giving written notice thereof to the Settlors, or to a surviving Settlor, or in the absence of any Settlor surviving, then to the Co-Trustee or in the absence of a Co-Trustee, then to all of the income beneficiaries of the trust at that time, or in the case of minor beneficiaries, to their natural guardians. Any resignation of a

Trustee shall become effective immediately following the transfer of all of the trust estate to the successor Trustee.

Section 3.03 <u>Successor Trustee</u>.

On the death of the first Settlor or in the event that either Settlor shall for any reason fail to qualify or cease to act as Trustee or become physically or mentally incapacitated, then the other of them shall act as sole Trustee hereunder. In the event that said sole Trustee shall for any reason fail to qualify or cease to act as Trustee, Settlors appoint ROGER DODGER to act as successor Trustee.

The surviving spouse may name successor, additional, and replacement Trustees and may remove any person acting or nominated to act as Trustee with respect to any trust (including a trust no longer revocable by a Settlor) by a signed writing delivered to such person.

With respect to this trust and any trust created hereunder, the last named Trustee shall have the power to designate a successor Trustee.

If all of the above-named Trustees fail to qualify or cease to act as Trustee and there is no other designated successor Trustee, any of the beneficiaries may petition a court of competent jurisdiction to appoint a Trustee to administer this trust or any trust created hereunder.

Any successor Trustee appointed herein shall succeed as Trustee with like effect as though originally named as such herein. All authority and powers conferred upon the original Trustee hereunder shall pass to any successor Trustee.

Section 3.04 <u>Trustee Provisions (Miscellaneous)</u>.

No individual Trustee shall be liable for any mistake or error in judgment in the administration of the trust herein created except for such Trustee's willful misconduct or gross negligence.

Any Co-Trustee named hereunder shall have the right to execute a special power of attorney in favor of the other Co-Trustee so as to allow the other Trustee to act alone with regard to the actions specified therein.

Section 3.05 <u>Trustee's Bond</u>.

No bond shall be required of any person named in this trust agreement as Trustee, or of any person appointed as Trustee in the manner specified herein, for the faithful performance of his duties as Trustee.

However, any beneficiary shall have the right to petition any court of competent jurisdiction to establish bond.

ARTICLE IV

Section 4.01 <u>Division of Trust Estate</u>.

Upon the death of the first Settlor, the trust estate shall be divided into three (3) separate and distinct trusts which shall be respectively designated and known as the "Survivor's Trust", the "Marital Trust", and the "Bypass Trust". In funding these three (3) trusts, the Trustee, with the surviving Settlor's consent, may allocate the surviving Settlor's interest in community property to either the Marital Trust or the Bypass Trust provided that the deceased Settlor's one-half ($^1/_2$) interest in other community property assets of equal value are allocated to the Survivor's Trust thus using the aggregate rather than the item approach to the funding of the trusts to the extent allowed by law.

A. <u>The Survivor's Trust</u>:

The Survivor's Trust shall consist of the surviving spouse's separate property and the surviving spouse's one-half ($^1/_2$) interest in the community property.

B. <u>The Marital Trust</u>:

The Marital Trust shall consist of the amount (referred to as the Marital Deduction Amount) equal to the minimum pecuniary amount necessary to entirely eliminate (or to reduce to the maximum extent possible) any federal estate tax at the predeceased spouse's death, taking into account:

(1) All deductions taken in determining the estate tax payable by reason of the predeceased spouse's death;

(2) The net value of all other property, whether or not it is given under this instrument and whether it passes at the time of the predeceased spouse's death or has passed before the predeceased spouse's death to or in trust for the surviving spouse, so that it is included in the predeceased spouse's gross estate and qualifies for the federal estate tax marital deduction; and

(3) All credits allowed for federal estate tax purposes other than any credit allowable under Internal Revenue Code Section 2011, to the extent that the credit exceeds any state death

taxes payable without regard to the availability of such credit, provided that no credit shall be taken into account in determining the size of the Marital Trust if such credit shall result in the disallowance of the marital deduction.

C. The Bypass Trust:

The Bypass Trust shall consist of the balance of the trust estate.

Section 4.02. Funding the Trusts.

A. The Trustee shall satisfy the amount so determined in cash or in kind, or partly in each, and shall allocate to the Marital Trust only assets that are eligible for the federal estate tax marital deduction. Assets allocated in kind shall be considered to satisfy this amount on the basis of their net fair market values as finally determined for federal estate tax purposes.

B. Assets qualifying for the federal estate tax marital deduction shall be transferred to the Marital Trust only to the extent that the transfer reduces the federal estate tax otherwise payable by reason of the predeceased spouse's death. No assets for which a credit for foreign death taxes is allowed under the federal estate tax law applicable to the predeceased spouse's estate shall be allocated to the Marital Trust, unless there is insufficient other property to fully fund the Marital Trust. The Trustee shall select property to satisfy the pecuniary amount constituting the Marital Trust, so that any appreciation or depreciation that has occurred in the value of trust property between the applicable valuation date and the date of allocation shall be fairly apportioned between the Marital Trust and the Bypass Trust.

C. The Settlors intend this marital deduction trust to qualify for the marital deduction under the applicable provisions of the Internal Revenue Code. The Settlors direct that the Trustee not take any action or exercise any power that will impair the marital deduction. This direction does not limit the Executor's power of election or non-election under Internal Revenue Code Section 2056(b)(7).

Section 4.03 Administration of Trusts During Life of Surviving Spouse.

A. The Survivor's Trust:

1. The Trustee shall pay to or apply for the benefit of the surviving spouse, during the surviving spouse's lifetime, quarter-annually

or at more frequent intervals, the entire net income from the Survivor's Trust. If the Trustee considers such income to be insufficient, the Trustee shall also pay to or apply for the benefit of the surviving spouse as much of the principal of the Survivor's Trust as the Trustee considers necessary for the surviving spouse's health, education, support, maintenance, comfort, welfare, or happiness. In addition, so long as the surviving spouse is competent the Trustee shall pay to the surviving spouse so much of the principal of the trust estate as the surviving spouse may, from time to time, request.

2. On the death of the surviving spouse, the Trustee shall distribute any remaining balance of the Survivor's Trust, including principal and accrued or undistributed income, to such one or more persons and entities, including the surviving spouse's own estate and on such terms and conditions, either outright or in trust, and in such proportions as the surviving spouse shall appoint by written instrument filed with the Trustee during the surviving spouse's lifetime or within sixty (60) days following the surviving spouse's death specifically referring to and exercising this power of appointment. An appointment may be revoked by the surviving spouse in a like manner unless otherwise provided in the instrument of appointment. If revocable, the last dated unrevoked instrument delivered to the Trustee within the period set forth above shall be effective at the surviving spouse's death. This power of appointment shall be exercisable by the surviving spouse alone and in all events.

3. On the death of the surviving spouse, the Trustee shall pay out of the principal of the Survivor's Trust the surviving spouse's last illness and funeral expenses and other obligations incurred for the surviving spouse's support and any estate or inheritance taxes attributable to the Survivor's Trust by reason of the surviving spouse's death. The balance of the Survivor's Trust, to the extent that it has not been otherwise appointed, shall be retained in trust or distributed as set forth.

B. Marital Trust:
  1. The Trustee shall pay to or apply for the benefit of the sur-
      viving spouse, during the surviving spouse's lifetime, quarter-
      annually or at more frequent intervals, the entire net income
      from the Marital Trust. The surviving spouse shall have the
      right to direct the Trustee in writing to convert any unproduc-
      tive property held in the marital deduction trust to productive
      property within a reasonable time, and the Trustee shall
      comply with this direction within a reasonable time after
      receipt of the directive. At the death of the surviving spouse,
      any income accumulated from the date of the last income dis-
      tribution through the date of the surviving spouse's death shall
      be distributed to the surviving spouse's estate.
  2. If the Trustee deems such income payments to be insufficient, the
      Trustee shall, from time to time, pay to or apply for the benefit of
      the surviving spouse such sums out of principal as the Trustee in
      the Trustee's discretion deems necessary for the surviving
      spouse's proper support, health, education, and maintenance.
  3. The Settlors request but do not require the Executor to make
      an election (referred to as the QTIP election) under Internal
      Revenue Code Section 2056(b)(7) if necessary to qualify all
      or part of the Marital Trust for the federal estate tax marital
      deduction. The Settlors recognize that the Marital Trust will
      not qualify for the marital deduction if the Executor does not
      make this election. In exercising this discretion, the Executor
      may consider all relevant factors, including (1) the potential
      benefits and detriments of reducing the federal estate tax on
      the predeceased spouse's estate and increasing the tax on the
      surviving spouse's estate and (2) the potential benefits of
      eliminating from the surviving spouse's gross estate the appre-
      ciation in value of the marital deduction share that may occur
      after the predeceased spouse's death and before the surviving
      spouse's death. The Executor's discretion shall be absolute,
      notwithstanding any beneficial or adverse effect on the prede-
      ceased spouse's estate, the surviving spouse's estate, or the
      beneficiaries of these estates. The Executor shall not incur

personal liability for exercising or not exercising this election, and the predeceased spouse's estate shall hold the Executor harmless against all claims with regard to the election. The discretion under this paragraph is not limited by the wording of the marital deduction intention clause.

4. On the death of the surviving spouse, the Trustee shall distribute the balance then remaining, if any, of the Marital Trust (including both principal and any accrued or undistributed income) to such one or more of the issue of the Settlors [Option 1: or to the spouses of said issue] [Option 2: or to any charitable institution] on such terms and conditions, either outright or in trust, as the surviving spouse shall appoint by a Will or other written instrument delivered to the Trustee and specifically referring to and exercising this power of appointment. This power of appointment shall be construed as a limited power of appointment.

5. On the death of the surviving spouse, the Marital Trust, to the extent it has not been effectively appointed, shall be retained in trust or distributed as set forth in Section 4.04.

6. If the surviving spouse effectively disclaims all the surviving spouse's beneficial interest in all or any portion of the Marital Trust, the Trustee shall distribute said trust, or the portion of the trust that corresponds to the disclaimed interest, to a trust designated and known as the "Disclaimer Bypass Trust" which shall be held, administered, and distributed in accordance with the provisions relating to the Bypass Trust except that the surviving spouse shall have no special power of appointment over the Disclaimer Bypass Trust.

C. Bypass Trust:

1. The Trustee shall pay to or for the surviving spouse as much of the income and principal, up to the whole of the trust, as the Trustee considers necessary for the surviving spouse's support, health, education, and maintenance to maintain at a minimum the surviving spouse's accustomed manner of living.

2. Upon the death of the surviving spouse, the Trustee shall distribute the balance then remaining, if any, of the Bypass Trust,

to such one or more of the issue of the Settlors [*Option 1*: or to the spouses of said issue] [*Option 2*: or to any charitable institution] and on such terms and conditions, either outright or in trust, as the surviving spouse shall appoint by a Will or other written instrument delivered to the Trustee specifically referring to and exercising this power of appointment. This power of appointment shall be construed as a limited power of appointment.

3. If the surviving spouse effectively disclaims all the surviving spouse's beneficial interest in all or any portion of the Bypass Trust, the Trustee shall distribute the trust, or the portion of the trust that corresponds to the disclaimed interest, according to the distribution provisions in Section 4.04.

4. On the death of the surviving spouse, the Bypass Trust, to the extent it has not been effectively appointed, shall be retained in trust or distributed as set forth in Section 4.04.

D. Provisions Common to Survivor's, Marital, and Bypass Trusts:

1. In making distributions to the surviving spouse for his or her support, health, education, and maintenance the Trustee shall be mindful of the fact that the primary concern of the Settlors is the welfare of the surviving spouse and that the interests of all remainder beneficiaries shall be subordinate to those of the surviving spouse. Moreover, in making said distributions, the Trustee need not take into account any other income or resources of the surviving spouse available for these purposes.

2. Until the death of the surviving spouse, the Trustee shall have no duty to diversify assets with respect to the Settlors' residence or any other real property of the trust estate utilized by the Settlors for their personal use or enjoyment.

Section 4.04 Disposition of Trusts after Death of Surviving Spouse.

Upon the death of the surviving spouse, the Trustee shall hold, administer and distribute the Survivor's Trust, the Marital Trust, and the Bypass Trust to the extent they have not been effectively appointed, as follows:

A. The Trustee shall distribute all items of tangible personal property described in any dated, and signed instructions that the Settlors, or either of them, leave in their safe deposit box, with this trust, or Will, or with other important papers in accordance with any such instructions. It is the Settlors' intention that any such written instructions shall qualify as an amendment to this trust. If such instructions fail to so qualify, then such instructions shall be deemed precatory and not mandatory and the Settlors request, but do not legally require, that the Trustee distribute such property in accordance with said instructions. If there are more than one set of instructions which contain conflicting provisions, the last-dated instructions shall control as to those provisions which conflict. Any distributions to the same person or entity on more than one set of instructions shall be deemed to be conflicting and not intended to supplement each other unless a contrary intention is specifically stated.

The balance of any tangible personal property shall be distributed to the Settlors' child, ROGER DODGER, if he is then living and, if not, to his children.

The Trustee shall pay from the trust estate any storage, packing, shipping, delivery, insurance, and other charges relating to the distribution of property and treat these payments as an administration expense.

The gift of tangible personal property shall be tax-free.

B.   The Trustee shall distribute the balance of the trust estate, as then constituted, to the Settlors' son, ROGER DODGER, if he survives the surviving Settlor and, if not, to his issue, by right of representation.

C.   If any distributee to whom the Trustee is to make distribution is under the age of twenty-five (25) years at the time, the Trustee shall either retain the property as custodian or select another to whom to distribute the property, as custodian, for the distributee under the California Uniform Transfers to Minors Act, with the custodianship to continue until the distributee attains age 25 or the time of termination of all present beneficial interests of the distributee in this trust, whichever event occurs first, unless the Trustee in the Trustee's absolute discretion believes the use of a custodianship would not be practical because of the amount or purposes of the distribution or for other reason. The Trustee shall not be liable to any beneficiary for the acts or omissions of a custodian selected by the Trustee so long as the Trustee's selection of the custodian is made in good faith.

Section 4.05 <u>Gift to Custodian</u>.

If any distributee for whom no other trust is established hereunder to whom the Trustee is to distribute income or principal is under the age of twenty-five (25) at the time, the Trustee shall either retain the property as custodian or select another to whom to distribute the property, as custodian, for the distributee under the California Uniform Transfers to Minors Act, with the custodianship to continue until the distributee attains age 25 years or the time of termination of all present beneficial interests of the distributee in this trust, whichever event occurs first, unless the Trustee in the Trustee's absolute discretion believes the use of a custodianship would not be practical because of the amount or purposes of the distribution or for other reason.

Section 4.06 <u>Ultimate Distribution</u>.

If, at any time, before full distribution of the trust estate, both Settlors and all of the issue of the Settlors are deceased and no other disposition of the trust estate is directed by this instrument, the Trustee shall distribute the balance of the trust estate, in equal shares, as follows:

A. One-half ($^1/_2$) to the heirs of the predeceased spouse, their identities and respective shares to be determined as though the predeceased spouse's death had then occurred and according to the laws of the State of California then in effect relating to the succession of separate property not acquired from a parent, grandparent, or previously deceased spouse.

B. One-half ($^1/_2$) to the heirs of the surviving spouse, their identities and respective shares to be determined as though the surviving spouse's death had then occurred and according to the laws of the State of California then in effect relating to the succession of separate property not acquired from a parent, grandparent, or previously deceased spouse.

ARTICLE V

Section 5.01 <u>Powers and Authorities of Trustee.</u>

The Trustee shall have all powers set out below with respect to all property and funds of the trust or trusts being administered under this instrument: [In addition, the Trustee may apply to any court of competent jurisdiction for such additional powers as may be appropriate to the orderly and effective administration of any trust created hereunder.]

1. To sell (for cash or on credit), exchange, purchase, and retain assets; to improve, alter, lease (even beyond the period of the trust), partition, and otherwise deal with and manage trust property; and to invest and reinvest in preferred or common stocks, bonds, mortgages, investment company shares, money market and mutual (including index) funds, common trust funds maintained by the Trustee, and any other property, real or personal; and the Trustee is not limited by legal restrictions on investment by fiduciaries.

2. To borrow money; to exercise all rights with respect to securities and other property; and to hold title in the name of a nominee or in a manner that will pass title by delivery or otherwise facilitate proper administration.

3. To employ and compensate (from the trust) accountants, lawyers, investment and tax advisors, agents and others, all as reasonable and appropriate (including by delegation) to aid in the management, administration, and protection of the trust estate.

4. To make distributions or allocations in cash or in kind, including undivided interests, by pro rata or non pro rata division, or any combination of these ways in the Trustee's discretion.

5. To make any payments or distributions (except as otherwise required herein) to a beneficiary directly, to a beneficiary's conservator or guardian (of the person or property), to any person deemed suitable by the Trustee, or by direct payment or application in a manner that will appropriately benefit the beneficiary.

6. To hold securities in a brokerage account in street name.

Section 5.02 <u>Principal and Income</u>.

Except as otherwise specifically provided in this trust agreement, the determination of all matters with respect to what is principal and income of the trust estate and the apportionment and allocation of receipts and expenses between these accounts shall be governed by the provisions of the California Revised Uniform Principal and Income Act from time to time existing. Any such matter not provided for either in this trust agreement or in the California Revised Uniform Principal and Income Act shall be determined by the Trustee in good faith in accordance with generally accepted accounting principles and due regard for the rights of the remainderman.

ARTICLE VI

Section 6.01 <u>Spendthrift Clause</u>.

No interest in the income of principal of any trust created under this instrument shall be voluntarily or involuntarily anticipated, assigned, encumbered, or subjected to creditor's claims or legal process before actual receipt by the beneficiary.

If the creditor of any beneficiary who is entitled to any distributions from a trust established under this instrument (other than from any marital deduction trust requiring the distribution of all income or any qualified Subchapter S Trust) attempts by any means to subject to the satisfaction of his or her claim that beneficiary's interest in any distribution, then, notwithstanding any other provision in this instrument, the distribution set aside for that beneficiary shall be disposed of, until the release of the writ of attachment or garnishment or other process, as follows:

1. The Trustee shall pay to or apply for the benefit of that beneficiary all sums that the Trustee, in the Trustee's discretion, determines to be necessary for the reasonable support, health, education (including study at an institution of higher learning or vocational school), and maintenance of the beneficiary according to his or her accustomed mode of life; and

2. The portion of the distribution that the Trustee determines to exceed the amount necessary for the health, education (including study at an institution of higher learning or vocational school), and support shall, in the Trustee's discretion, either be added to and become principal in whole or in part, or be paid to or applied for the benefit of the other beneficiaries then entitled to receive payments from any trust established

under this instrument, in proportion to their respective interests in the trust estate; or, if there are no other beneficiaries, the excess income may be paid to or applied for the benefit of the person or persons presumptively entitled to the next eventual interest, in proportion to their respective interests in the trust.

Section 6.02 <u>Payment to Minor</u>.

In any case where payment is made to a minor, the Trustee may make such payment directly to such minor as an allowance, or to the parent or guardian of such minor, or to any other person having the care and control of the minor, or with whom he may reside, and the receipt by any such person for any such payment shall be a complete discharge of the Trustee as to amounts so paid. In connection with this paragraph and with this trust agreement, the Trustee is specifically directed to consult with the guardians of the person of any child who is a beneficiary hereunder regarding his care, welfare, education, and needs. The Trustee is instructed to adopt the recommendations and advice of said guardians as to the welfare and needs of said children unless the Trustee, of his own knowledge, is aware of facts which would negate such advice.

ARTICLE VII

Section 7.01 <u>Trust Contest</u>

Except as otherwise provided in this trust, Settlors have intentionally and with full knowledge omitted to provide for their heirs. If any person who, if Settlors had died intestate, would be entitled to any part of the estate, shall either directly or indirectly, alone or in conjunction with any other person, claim in spite of this trust an intestate share in Settlors' estate, that person shall be given One Dollar ($1.00), and no more, in lieu of any other share or interest in this estate.

If any beneficiary under this trust in any manner, directly or indirectly, contests this trust or any of the trusts established herein or any of the provisions of any of said trusts in any legal proceeding that is designed to thwart Settlors' wishes as expressed in said trusts, any share or interest in this estate given to that contesting beneficiary under any of said trusts is revoked and shall be disposed of in the same manner provided herein as if that contesting beneficiary had predeceased Settlors without issue.

Section 7.02 <u>Jurisdiction</u>.

This trust is established by the Settlors and is hereby accepted by the Trustee under the laws of the State of California. All questions concerning its validity, construction, and administration shall be determined under the laws thereof.

The appropriate Superior Court of the State of California shall have jurisdiction for all the purposes set forth in Section 1138.1 of the California Probate Code. The Trustee may transfer the trust estate to any other state or any other jurisdiction outside the continental limits of the United States, if, in his sole discretion, it is deemed to be in the best interests of the beneficiaries hereunder. Should such a transfer of jurisdiction occur, the Trustee shall appoint a successor Trustee within such jurisdiction if the Trustee deems it advisable.

Section 7.03 <u>Definition of "Issue"</u>.

As used in this trust, the term "issue" shall include or exclude persons in accordance with rules for construing class gift terms under the California Probate Code as it exists at the date of this trust instrument; and distribution to issue or descendants shall be made as prescribed in California Probate Code Section 240 at the date of this instrument.

Section 7.04 <u>Gender and Number</u>.

As used in this trust agreement, the masculine, feminine, and neuter gender, and the singular or plural number shall be deemed to include the other whenever the context so indicates.

Section 7.05 <u>Invalidity of Provisions</u>.

Should any provision of this trust agreement be determined to be ineffective or invalid for any reason whatsoever, the other provisions hereof shall nevertheless remain in full force and effect.

ARTICLE VIII

Section 8.01 <u>Name of Trust</u>.

This trust shall be referred to as "**The ART AND ELLIE DODGER FAMILY TRUST**"

IN WITNESS WHEREOF, the Settlors and Trustee respectively have executed this trust agreement the day and year first above written.

SETTLORS:

_____

ART DODGER

_____

ELLIE DODGER

TRUSTEE:

_____

ART DODGER

_____

ELLIE DODGER

WITNESSES:

_____ residing at _____

_____ residing at _____

_____

State of _____

County of _____

On _____, 200_, before me, a Notary Public, personally appeared ART DODGER and ELLIE DODGER, personally known to me or proved to me on the basis of satisfactory evidence to be the person[s] whose name[s] is/are subscribed to the within instrument and acknowledged to me that he/she/they executed the same in his/her/their authorized capacity(ies), and that by his/her/their signature(s) on the instrument the person(s), or the entity upon behalf of which the person(s) acted, executed the instrument.

WITNESS my hand and official seal.

_____

APPENDIX G

This form is presented by way of example only.
Do not use this form without the advice of your attorney.

ADVANCE HEALTH CARE DIRECTIVE
[California Probate Code Section 4701]

[Name]

You have the right to give instructions about your own health care. You also have the right to name someone else to make health care decisions for you. This form lets you do either or both of these things. It also lets you express your wishes regarding donation of organs and the designation of your primary physician. If you use this form, you may complete or modify all or any part of it. You are free to use a different form.

Part 1 of this form is a power of attorney for health care. Part 1 lets you name another individual as agent to make health care decisions for you if you become incapable of making your own decisions or if you want someone else to make those decisions for you now even though you are still capable. You may also name an alternate agent to act for you if your first choice is not willing, able, or reasonably available to make decisions for you. (Your agent may not be an operator or employee of a community care facility or a residential care facility where you are receiving care, or your supervising health care provider or employee of the health care institution where you are receiving care, unless your agent is related to you or is a co-worker.)

Unless the form you sign limits the authority of your agent, your agent may make all health care decisions for you. This form has a place for you to limit the authority of your agent. You need not limit the authority of your agent if you wish to rely on your agent for all health care decisions that may have to be made. If you choose not to limit the authority of your agent, your agent will have the right to:

(a) Consent or refuse consent to any care, treatment, service, or procedure to maintain, diagnose, or otherwise affect a physical or mental condition.

(b) Select or discharge health care providers and institutions.

(c) Approve or disapprove diagnostic tests, surgical procedures, and programs of medication.

(d) Direct the provision, withholding, or withdrawal of artificial nutrition and hydration and all other forms of health care, including cardiopulmonary resuscitation.

(e) Make anatomical gifts, authorize an autopsy, and direct disposition of remains.

Part 2 of this form lets you give specific instructions about any aspect of your health care, whether or not you appoint an agent. Choices are provided for you to express your wishes regarding the provision, withholding, or withdrawal of treatment to keep you alive, as well as the provision of pain relief. Space is also provided for you to add to the choices you have made or for you to write out any additional wishes. If you are satisfied to allow your agent to determine what is best for you in making end-of-life decisions, you need not fill out Part 2 of this form.

Part 3 of this form lets you express an intention to donate your bodily organs and tissues following your death.

Part 4 of this form lets you designate a physician to have primary responsibility for your health care.

After completing this form, sign and date the form at the end. The form must be signed by two (2) qualified witnesses or acknowledged before a Notary Public. Give a copy of the signed and completed form to your physician, or any other health care providers you may have, and to any health care agents you have named. You should talk to the person you have named as agent to make sure that he or she understands your wishes and is willing to take the responsibility.

You have the right to revoke this Advance Health Care Directive or replace this form at any time.

PART 1
POWER OF ATTORNEY FOR HEALTH CARE

(1.1) DESIGNATION OF AGENT: I, _____, designate _____, of _____ (Telephone: _____), as my agent to make health care decisions for me.

OPTIONAL: If I revoke my agent's authority or if my agent it not willing, able, or reasonably available to make a health care decision for me, I designate as my first agent:

First Alternate Agent:

Address:

Telephone:

OPTIONAL: If I revoke the authority of my agent and first alternate agent or if neither is willing, able, or reasonably available to make a health care decision for me, I designate as my second alternate agent:

Second Alternate Agent:

Address:

Telephone:

(1.2) AGENT'S AUTHORITY: My agent is authorized to make all health care decisions for me, including decisions to provide, withhold, or withdraw artificial nutrition and hydration and all other forms of health care to keep me alive, except as I state here:

(1.3) WHEN AGENT'S AUTHORITY BECOMES EFFECTIVE: My agent's authority becomes effective when my primary physician determines that I am unable to make my own health care decisions unless I mark the following box.

If I mark this box [ ], my agent's authority to make health care decisions for me takes effect immediately.

(1.4) AGENT'S OBLIGATION: My agent shall make health care decisions for me in accordance with this power of attorney for health care, any instructions I give in Part 2 of this form, and my other wishes to the extent known to my agent. To the extent my wishes are unknown, my agent shall make health care decisions for me in accordance with what my agent determines to be in my best interest. In determining my best interest, my agent shall consider my personal values to the extent known to my agent.

(1.5) AGENT'S POST–DEATH AUTHORITY: My agent is authorized to make anatomical gifts, authorize an autopsy, and direct disposition of my remains, except as I state here or in Part 3 of this form:

(1.6) NOMINATION OF CONSERVATOR: If a conservator of my person needs to be appointed for me by a court, I nominate the agent designated in this form. If that agent is not willing, able, or reasonably available to act as conservator, I nominate the alternate agents whom I have named, in the order designated.

PART 2
INSTRUCTIONS FOR HEALTH CARE

If you fill out this part of the form, you may strike any wording you do not want.

(2.1) END-OF-LIFE DECISIONS: I direct that my health care providers and others involved in my care provide, withhold, or withdraw treatment in accordance with the choice I have marked below:

❑ (a) Choice Not to Prolong Life: I do not want my life to be prolonged if (1) I have an incurable and irreversible condition that will result in my death within a relatively short time, (2) I become unconscious and, to a reasonable degree of medical certainty, I will not regain consciousness, or (3) the likely risks and burdens of treatment would outweigh the expected benefits, OR

❑ (b) Choice to Prolong Life: I want my life to be prolonged as long as possible within the limits of generally accepted health care standards.

(2.2) RELIEF FROM PAIN: Except as I state in the following space, I direct that treatment for alleviation of pain or discomfort be provided at all times, even if it hastens my death:

(2.3) OTHER WISHES: (If you do not agree with any of the optional choices above and wish to write your own, or if you wish to add to the instructions you have given above, you may do so here.) I direct that:

PART 3
DONATION OF ORGANS AT DEATH (OPTIONAL)

(3.1) Upon my death (mark applicable box):

❑   (a) I give any needed organs, tissues, or parts, OR

❑   (b) I give the following organs, tissues, or parts only:

❑   (c) My gift is for the following purposes (strike any of the following you do not want):

(1) Transplant

(2) Therapy

(3) Research

(4) Education

PART 4
PRIMARY PHYSICIAN(OPTIONAL)

(4.1) I designate the following physician as my primary physician:

Name:_____

Address: _____

Telephone: _____

OPTIONAL: If the physician I have designated above is not willing, able, or reasonably available to act as my primary physician, I designate the following physician as my primary physician:

Name:_____

Address: _____

Telephone: _____

PART 5

(5.1) EFFECT OF COPY: A copy of this form has the same effect as the original.

(5.2) SIGNATURE:

Executed this __ day of _____, [Year], at _____, California.

_____

[PRINCIPAL]

(5.3) STATEMENT OF WITNESSES: I declare under penalty of perjury under the laws of the State of California (1) that the individual who signed or acknowledged this Advance Health Care Directive is personally known to me, or that the individual's identity was proven to me by convincing evidence, (2) that the individual signed or acknowledged this advance directive in my presence, (3) that the individual appears to be of sound mind and under no duress, fraud, or undue influence, (4) that I am not a person appointed as agent by this advance directive, and (5) that I am not the individual's health care provider, an employee of the individual's health care provider, the operator of a community care facility, an employee of an operator of a community care facility, the operator of a residential care facility for the elderly, nor an employee of an operator of a residential care facility for the elderly.

_____

Witness

_____

[Address]

_____

Witness

_____

[Address]

ADDITIONAL STATEMENT OF WITNESSES: At least one of the above witnesses must also sign the following declaration:
I further declare under penalty of perjury under the laws of California that I am not related to the individual executing this Advance Health Care Directive by blood, marriage, or adoption, and to the best of my knowledge, I am not entitled to any part of the individual's estate upon his or her death under a will now existing or by operation of law.

_____

Witness

_____

Witness

PART 6
SPECIAL WITNESS REQUIREMENT

(6.1) The following statement is required only if you are a patient in a skilled nursing facility—a health care facility that provides the following basic services: skilled nursing care and supportive care to patients whose primary need is for availability of skilled nursing care on an extended basis. The patient advocate or ombudsman must sign the following statement:

STATEMENT OF PATIENT ADVOCATE OR OMBUDSMAN

I declare under penalty of perjury under the laws of California that I am a patient advocate or ombudsman as designated by the State Department of Aging and that I am serving as a witness as required by Probate Code Section 4675.

Signature: _____

APPENDIX H

This form is presented by way of example only.
Do not use this form without the advice of your attorney.

STATEMENT OF DESIRES, SPECIAL PROVISIONS, AND LIMITATIONS FOR DURABLE POWER OF ATTORNEY FOR HEALTH CARE

If I develop any incurable, progressive, or degenerative disease stated to be terminal with respect to outcome (not with respect to time) and no cure is available and treatment only prolongs dying, I request that my physician follow my guide regarding life support and life-sustaining intervention listed below. If any desires are not known and life-sustaining or life-support procedures are utilized in an emergency situation, I request that my desires be respected and followed once they are known to my professional care team. I do not want to be kept alive in a vegetative state.

LIFE SUPPORT

	MY DESIRES		
	YES	NO	UNCERTAIN
Pacemaker—any device that substitutes for the normal heartbeat	❏	❏	❏
Peritoneal Dialysis; Kidney Dialysis—alternative means of filtering poisons from the body when the kidneys fail	❏	❏	❏
Respirator—a breathing machine attached to a tube inserted into the lungs through the nose or mouth	❏	❏	❏
Cardiopulmonary resuscitation (CPR)—intervention given by man, machine, or drugs when the heart and/or lungs stop working	❏	❏	❏

LIFE -PROLONGING OR LIFE-SUSTAINING PROCEDURES

	MY DESIRES		
	YES	NO	UNCERTAIN
Feeding tube for food or fluid—a tube placed into the stomach or bowel to give fluid and/or nutrition	❏	❏	❏
Intravenous (IV)—tubes for feeding and hydration	❏	❏	❏
Antibiotics—to treat pneumonia or any other infections	❏	❏	❏
Cancer Therapy—radiation: x-ray treatments given for tumors or cancers; chemotherapy: cancer medicine given by mouth or intravenously	❏	❏	❏
Transfusion—blood or blood products given into the vein	❏	❏	❏
Medical Treatment—diagnostic procedures and tests; further tests and procedures to monitor my failing condition	❏	❏	❏
Surgery—an operation only if it provides for my comfort and dignity	❏	❏	❏
Paramedic—for transport to an acute hospital with CPR in progress	❏	❏	❏
Uniform Gift Act—organ transplant donating body parts; specify parts, if usable	❏	❏	❏
Autopsy—complete or selective, to confirm my diagnosis (check one)	❏	❏	❏

I consent to participate in research, i.e., chemical studies, drug studies, and procedures approved by a Research and Human Subject Review Committee, before or after my death.

Consent may be given by my Attorney-in-Fact	❏	❏	❏

OTHER CONCERNS OR CORRECTIONS

_____

_____

MY WISHES:

1. Caring and supportive nursing and medical care to relieve pain and suffering including narcotics to relieve pain even if respiration is depressed.
2. Food and fluids to be offered as long as I am conscious to take them by mouth and then moist sponges to moisten my lips to relieve the sensation of dehydration.

Signature: _____ Date: _____

APPENDIX I

This form is presented by way of example only.
Do not use this form without the advice of your attorney.

DIRECTIVE TO PHYSICIANS

[California Health and Safety Code §7186.5]

I, _____, being of sound mind, willfully and voluntarily make known my desire that my life shall not be artificially prolonged under the circumstances set forth below, and I do hereby declare:

If at any time I should have an incurable and irreversible condition that has been diagnosed by two (2) physicians and that will result in my death within a relatively short time without the administration of life-sustaining treatment or has produced an irreversible coma or persistent vegetative state, and I am no longer able to make decisions regarding my medical treatment, I direct my attending physician, pursuant to the Natural Death Act of California, to withhold or withdraw treatment, including artificially administered nutrition and hydration, that only prolongs the process of dying or the irreversible coma or persistent vegetative state and is not necessary for my comfort or to alleviate pain.

If I have been diagnosed as pregnant, and that diagnosis is known to my physician, this declaration shall have no force or effect during my pregnancy.

Signed this _____ day of _____, [Year]

_____
[Signature]
[Address]

The declarant voluntarily signed this writing in my presence. I am not a health care provider, an employee of a health care provider, the operator of a community care facility, an employee of an operator of a community care facility, the operator of a residential care facility for the elderly, or an employee of an operator of a residential care facility for the elderly.

_____   _____
[Witness]   [Address]

The declarant voluntarily signed this writing in my presence. I am not entitled to any portion of the estate of the declarant upon his or her death under any will or codicil thereto of the declarant now existing or by operation of law. I am not a health care provider, an employee of a health care provider, the operator of a community care facility, an employee of an operator of a community care facility, the operator of a residential care facility for the elderly, or an employee of an operator of a residential care facility for the elderly

                    _____

                    [Witness]

                    [Address]

APPENDIX J

When recorded, return to:

UNIFORM STATUTORY FORM POWER OF ATTORNEY
[California Probate Code §4401]

NOTICE: THE POWERS GRANTED BY THIS DOCUMENT ARE BROAD AND SWEEPING. THEY ARE EXPLAINED IN THE UNIFORM STATUTORY FORM POWER OF ATTORNEY ACT (CALIFORNIA PROBATE CODE SECTIONS 4400-4465). IF YOU HAVE ANY QUESTIONS ABOUT THESE POWERS, OBTAIN COMPETENT LEGAL ADVICE. THIS DOCUMENT DOES NOT AUTHORIZE ANYONE TO MAKE MEDICAL AND OTHER HEALTH-CARE DECISIONS FOR YOU. YOU MAY REVOKE THIS POWER OF ATTORNEY IF YOU LATER WISH TO DO SO.

I, _____, a resident of _____ County, appoint _____ whose address and telephone number are:

as my agent (attorney-in-fact) to act for me in any lawful way with respect to the following initialed subjects:

TO GRANT ALL OF THE FOLLOWING POWERS, INITIAL THE LINE IN FRONT OF (O) AND IGNORE THE LINES IN FRONT OF THE OTHER POWERS.

TO GRANT ONE OR MORE, BUT FEWER THAN ALL, OF THE FOLLOWING POWERS, INITIAL THE LINE IN FRONT OF EACH POWER YOU ARE GRANTING.

TO WITHHOLD A POWER, DO NOT INITIAL THE LINE IN FRONT OF IT. YOU MAY, BUT NEED NOT, CROSS OUT EACH POWER WITHHELD.

INITIAL

_____ (A) Real property transactions.

_____ (B) Tangible personal property transactions.

_____ (C) Stock and bond transactions.

_____ (D) Commodity and option transactions.

_____ (E) Banking and other financial institution transactions.

_____ (F) Business operating transactions.

_____ (G) Insurance and annuity transactions.

_____ (H) Estate, trust, and other beneficiary transactions.

_____ (I) Claims and litigation.

_____ (J) Personal and family maintenance.

_____ (K) Benefits from social security, Medicare, Medicaid, or other governmental programs, or civil or military service.

_____ (L) Retirement plan transactions.

_____ (M) Tax matters.

_____ (N) To make transfers into, to revoke, to amend, or to withdraw funds from a revocable trust of which the principal is a Settlor for the purpose of reducing taxes or accomplishing actions that a reasonable person would take to achieve the overall objectives of the trust without avoidable tax consequences and in such a way that the Settlor's dispositive plan is not substantially altered.

_____ (O) **ALL OF THE POWERS LISTED ABOVE.**

[You need not initial any other lines if you initial Line O.]

_____ The Principal's agent is hereby authorized in the agent's sole discretion to make gifts of the Principal's property to any one or more of the Principal's issue to the extent of the Principal's annual exclusion(s) for federal gift tax purposes so as to reduce the federal estate tax due with respect to the Principal's estate. Except as provided in the preceding sentence, nothing herein shall authorize the Principal's agent to change the beneficiary provisions of the Principal's estate planning. The Principal's agent is hereby authorized to withdraw funds from a revocable trust of which the Principal is the Settlor for the purpose of said gifts.

SPECIAL INSTRUCTIONS

ON THE FOLLOWING LINES YOU MAY GIVE SPECIAL INSTRUCTIONS LIMITING OR EXTENDING THE POWERS GRANTED TO YOUR AGENT.

_____

_____

APPOINTMENT OF ALTERNATE AGENT

If for any reason _____ is unwilling or unable to continue to serve as agent, the following person shall instead serve:

NAME:
ADDRESS:
TELEPHONE:

In such case, one of the following documents shall be attached to this durable power of attorney: a resignation or declination to serve signed by the original agent or successor agent; a written and signed opinion from a licensed physician that the original agent or successor agent is physically or mentally incapable of serving; a certified court order as to the incapacity, inability, or termination of authority of the original agent or successor agent to serve; or a certified death certificate of the original agent or successor agent. Third parties who deal with the successor agents shall be entitled to rely on the original power of attorney instrument with any such document attached.

OPTION 1:
[UNLESS YOU DIRECT OTHERWISE ABOVE, THIS POWER OF ATTORNEY IS EFFECTIVE IMMEDIATELY AND WILL CONTINUE UNTIL IT IS REVOKED.

THIS POWER OF ATTORNEY WILL CONTINUE TO BE EFFECTIVE EVEN THOUGH I BECOME INCAPACITATED. Strike the preceding sentence if you do not want this power of attorney to continue if you become incapacitated.]

OPTION 2:
[THIS POWER OF ATTORNEY SHALL BECOME EFFECTIVE ONLY ON MY SUBSEQUENT INCAPACITY.

I will conclusively be deemed incapacitated for the purposes of this instrument when my agent receives a written and signed opinion from a licensed physician, practicing in the area in which I reside, that I am either physically or mentally incapable of managing my own affairs. Said instrument, when received, shall be attached to this document. Third parties may rely on my agent's authority without further evidence of incapacity when this instrument is presented with such a physician's statement attached pursuant to Probate Code §4405.]

I agree that any third party who receives a copy of this document may act under it. Revocation of the power of attorney is not effective as to a third party until the third party has actual knowledge of the revocation. I agree to indemnify the third party for any claims that arise against the third party because of reliance on this power of attorney.

Signed this _____ day of _____, 2003.

_____

Social Security Number:

_____

State of _____
County of _____

On _____ 2003, before me the undersigned notary public, personally appeared _____ personally known to me or proved to me on the basis of satisfactory evidence to be the person whose name is subscribed to the within instrument and acknowledged to me that he/she executed the same in his/her author-ized capacity(ies), and that by his/her signature(s) on the instrument the person(s), or the entity upon behalf of which the person(s) acted, executed the instrument.

WITNESS my hand and official seal.

_____

BY ACCEPTING OR ACTING UNDER THE APPOINTMENT, THE AGENT ASSUMES THE FIDUCIARY AND OTHER LEGAL RESPONSIBILITIES OF AN AGENT.

APPENDIX K

This form is presented by way of example only.
Do not use this form without the advice of your attorney.

COMMUNITY PROPERTY AFFIDAVIT

We, _____ and _____, husband and wife, hereby declare that all of the property which we now hold or hereafter acquire in our names as joint tenants or tenants in common or which we hold as Co-Trustees of a living trust of which we are the Settlors that was formerly held in our names as joint tenants or tenants in common is hereby transmuted by us to community property with the exception of any bank or savings accounts standing in our names as joint tenants.

EXECUTED this ___ day of ___, [Year], at _____, California.

_____   _____
[Husband]   [Wife]

APPENDIX L

This form is presented by way of example only.
Do not use this form without the advice of your attorney.

NOMINATION OF CONSERVATOR

I, _____, hereby nominate the following individuals, in the order in which they are named, as the Conservator of my person:

[First Nominee]

[Second Nominee]

I, _____, hereby nominate the following individuals, in the order in which they are named, as the Conservator of my estate:

[First Nominee]

[Second Nominee]

In the event the first nominee fails to qualify or ceases to act as my Conservator, I nominate the second nominee as Conservator to act in his or her stead.

No bond shall be required of any of the above-nominated Conservators.

This Nomination of Conservator hereby revokes all prior nominations.

DATED: _____   _____

                                                    [Declarant]

APPENDIX M

This form is presented by way of example only.
Do not use this form without the advice of your attorney.

CONFIDENTIAL CLIENT QUESTIONNAIRE
(ASSET INFORMATION)

NAME: _____

SPOUSE'S NAME: _____

ESTIMATED VALUE OF GROSS ESTATE: _____

ASSETS

    A. Real Property

For each parcel of real property owned by you, please attach a copy of the deed and provide the following information:

        Address: _____

        How Title Held: _____

        Estimated Fair Market Value: _____

        Present Encumbrance: _____

        Name of Lender(s): _____

        (Please attach additional sheets if you own more than one parcel of real property.)

    B. Corporate Securities

[If your securities are held in a brokerage account, you may simply attach a copy of a recent statement.]

Name of Security	Value
_____	$_____
_____	$_____
_____	$_____

How Title Held: _____

Location of Certificates: _____

Name and Address of Stockbroker: _____

    C. Cash

        Bank Account/

Location	*How Held	Approx. Balance
_____	_____	$_____
_____	_____	$_____
_____	_____	$_____
_____	_____	$_____
_____	_____	$_____
_____	_____	$_____
_____	_____	$_____

*How Bank Accounts Held (i.e., joint tenancy, individually, tenants in common)

D. Life Insurance

For each life insurance policy owned, please provide the following:

Company/ Policy No.	Face Value	Beneficiary(ies)	Owner(s)
_____	$_____	_____	_____
_____	$_____	_____	_____
_____	$_____	_____	_____
_____	$_____	_____	_____

E. Personal Property

Please state the approximate value of all tangible personal property owned by you and its location:

_____

Among your tangible personal property, are there any antiques or objects of art? [Yes/No] _____

F. Retirement/Pension Plans

For each retirement, pension, or profit-sharing plan, please state the following:

Employer: _____

Type of Plan: _____

Designated Beneficiary(ies): _____

_____

_____

Name and Address of Plan Administrator: _____

_____

_____

G. Client-Owned Business
   Name: _____ Type: _____
      Other owners: _____
      Is there a buy–sell agreement? _____
H. Partnership Interests
   Name of Partnership: _____
      Names of Other Partners: _____
      _____
I. Unsecured Liabilities (over $2,500)
   Amount Owed   Payee
      $ _____   _____
      $ _____   _____
J. Other Assets [i.e., interest in lawsuit, copyrights, patents, mineral rights]

   _____

   _____

   _____

K. Safe Deposit Box: _____ Location: _____
   Location of Key: _____
L. Accountant
Name and address of your accountant and/or tax adviser:

   _____

   _____

   _____

M. Do you have a beneficial interest in a trust? If so, please provide a copy of the trust.

N. Do you expect to inherit property in the foreseeable future? If so, please describe what you expect to inherit and from whom.

O. Have you made gifts of over $11,000 to anyone? If yes, please provide the name of the person, the date of the gift, and the value of the gift.

Did you file gift tax returns?

P. Please indicate any special burial or funeral instructions you wish your Executor to know about.

APPENDIX N

This form is presented by way of example only.
Do not use this form without the advice of your attorney.

CONFIDENTIAL CLIENT QUESTIONNAIRE
(FAMILY INFORMATION)

DATED: _____

NAME: _____ SPOUSE'S NAME: _____

HOME ADDRESS: _____

_____

Home telephone number: _____Work: _____

Your birthdate: _____Spouse's birthdate: _____

Your Social Security number: _____

Spouse's Social Security number: _____

Both spouses U.S. citizens? _____ If not, please indicate citizenship:

NAMES OF CHILDREN:
(Include birthdates, marital status, telephone numbers, and addresses)

NAMES OF CHILDREN OF SPOUSE:
(Include birthdates, marital status, telephone numbers, and addresses)

NAMES OF GRANDCHILDREN:
(Include birthdates and addresses, and identify parent)

NAMES OF YOUR PARENTS, IF LIVING: _____

_____

NAMES OF YOUR SPOUSE'S PARENTS, IF LIVING: _____

_____

If you have neither living parents nor children, please give the name, relationship, and address of your next of kin and those of your spouse:

APPENDIX O

CHECKLIST OF THINGS TO DISCUSS
WITH YOUR OWN CLEVER ATTORNEY

1. Should you have a will or a living trust?
2. If you are married, do you need:
   A. A tax savings trust (bypass trust)? (Probably, if the estate of you and your spouse is likely to exceed $1,500,000.)
   B. A QTIP trust? (Probably, if you want to control what happens to your property after both you and your spouse are gone.)
   C. A special power of appointment? (Probably, if you want to give your spouse the ability to control what happens to your property after your death.)
   D. A QDOT trust? (Probably, if either of you is not a U.S. citizen and either of you has assets worth over $1,500,000.)
   E. A community property affidavit? (Probably, if you live in a community property state and own appreciated property.)
   F. A durable general power of attorney? (Probably, if you have a living trust or want an inexpensive alternative to a conservatorship in the event of a temporary disability.)
3. If you have children:
   A. How do you want to leave bequests to minor children?
      (1) To a guardian?
      (2) To a trustee?
      (3) To a custodian under the Uniform Transfers to Minors Act?
   B. Do you want to make annual exclusion gifts to your children? If so, how do you want to leave the gifts?
      (1) To a custodian under the Uniform Transfers to Minors Act?
      (2) To a minor's trust?

(3) To a Crummey trust?

(4) To a Qualified State Tuition Program?

C. Should you establish a qualified personal residence trust? (Possibly, if you don't mind a bit of a gamble.)

4. If you have grandchildren, do you want to create a generation-skipping trust? (Probably, if you are interested in saving your grandchildren taxes.)

5. Should you execute the following documents:

A. A health care directive? (Probably, if there is someone to whom you are willing to delegate your health care decisions.)

B. A living will? (Probably, if there is no one to whom you are willing to delegate your health care decisions and if you don't want your life artificially prolonged.)

C. A nomination of conservator? (Probably, especially if you don't have a living trust.)

6. If you are charitably minded: Should you make gifts of appreciated property to charity? Should you establish, during your life or at death, a charitable remainder trust? Or contribute to a pooled income fund?

7. If you have an IRA or other retirement plans, you should:

A. Review all beneficiary designations.

B. Determine whether a Roth IRA is for you.

A SIMPLIFIED
GLOSSARY OF TERMS

Author's note: Following are nontechnical, nonwindy definitions of the concepts covered in this book. They are accurate as far as they go. But if you really want full-blown, detailed definitions, you should consult *Black's Law Dictionary* or other more definitive legal texts.

Alaskan trust: an irrevocable trust, usually for the benefit of the person who set it up, that is exempt from creditors' claims arising after its creation.

Alternate valuation date: for estate tax purposes, the date six months after the date of death upon which assets may be valued.

Annual exclusion: up to $11,000 (subject to periodic upward adjustments) you can give away annually to each of any number of people, tax-free.

Basis, tax: what you paid for an asset (in the case of real property, less depreciation plus any improvements).

Beneficiary, life insurance: the person (or entity) who, upon the death of the insured, is entitled to receive the insurance proceeds.

Beneficiary, trust: the person(s) entitled to receive distributions from a trust.

Bond: a written undertaking by a bonding company to protect the estate from losses resulting from theft by the trustee, conservator, or guardian.

Bypass trust: a trust, containing up to the exemption amount, that escapes tax in the surviving spouse's estate.

Capital gains tax: income tax you pay on the gain (the difference between an asset's basis and its sales price) when you sell an asset.

Certification, legal: attestation by the state bar association that an attorney has qualified as an expert in a particular field.

Charitable lead trust: a trust, eventually passing to charity that pays you or your family the income from the charity's investment fund.

Charitable remainder trust: a trust, eventually passing to charity, that pays you or your family members a set amount of money each year.

Community property: property acquired during your marriage other than by gift or inheritance.

Community property affidavit: a document confirming that all property held in the name of you and your spouse is community property.

Conservatee: the person for whom a conservatorship is established.

Conservator of the estate: the court-appointed person (or entity) having the responsibility for the conservatee's financial affairs.

Conservator of the person: the court-appointed person (or entity) having the responsibility for the conservatee's personal care.

Corporation: a business entity in which the liability of its shareholders is limited to the value of its assets.

Cristofani trust: a variation on the Crummey trust that is sufficiently difficult to explain that you will just have to refer to the end of Chapter 9.

Crummey trust: a trust, usually established for the benefit of a child, that is not required to terminate when the child reaches age twenty-one.

Directive to physicians: a document directed to your doctor stating that you do not want your life artificially prolonged.

Disclaimer: a document in which you give up your right to all or part of an inheritance.

Durable power of attorney for health care: a document in which you appoint someone to make health care decisions for you in the event you are incapable of doing so.

Durable power of attorney, general: a document that survives your incompetency and gives another person the right to conduct your financial affairs.

Educational IRA (Individual Retirement Account): a fund for the education of your children to which contributions are not deductible but from which distributions for educational purposes are tax-free.

Estate taxes: taxes imposed by the federal government at your death based on the value of the property in your estate.

Executor, executrix: the person (or entity) appointed by the court to administer your estate.

Exempt assets: assets not subject to creditors' claims.

Exemption, estate tax: the value of assets ($1,500,000 in 2004, increasing to $3,500,000 in 2009) you can give away at death free of estate taxes.

Exemption, gift tax: the value of assets ($1,000,000) you can give away during your life free of gift taxes.

Extraordinary fees: additional fees charged by the probate attorney, subject to court approval, for services not covered by the probate fee.

Fiscal year: a tax year, as distinguished from a calendar year, that can be chosen for income tax purposes after your death.

Fraudulent conveyance: a transfer of assets made primarily for the purpose of avoiding creditors' claims.

General partnership: a partnership in which all partners are liable for partnership obligations.

Generation-skipping trust: a trust into which you put up to $1,100,000 (subject to periodic upward adjustments) that will pass to your grandchildren without being taxed in your children's estates.

Gift taxes: taxes imposed by the federal government on lifetime transfers.

GRAT (grantor retained annuity trust): a trust into which the grantor transfers income-producing property, reserving an income interest for a stated number of years (based on a percentage of the original value of the trust) with the remainder usually passing to his or her children.

GRUT (grantor retained unitrust): a trust into which the grantor transfers income-producing property, reserving an income interest for a stated number of years (based on a percentage of the value of the trust calculated annually) with the remainder usually passing to his or her children.

Gross estate: the value of your entire estate undiminished by allowable deductions such as debts or administration expenses.

Guardian of the estate: the court-appointed person (or entity) having the responsibility for a minor's financial affairs.

Guardian of the person: the court-appointed person (or entity) having the responsibility for a minor's personal care.

Homestead exemption: the value of your home protected from creditors' claims.

IRA (Individual Retirement Account): a retirement account to which contributions are tax deductible and from which distributions are taxed.

Insured: the person whose death causes insurance proceeds to be payable to a named beneficiary.

Intestate succession: the manner in which your estate passes under state law if you die without a will.

Inventory and appraisal: the document filed in a probate, a conservatorship, or a guardianship proceeding that lists and values all assets of the estate.

Investigator, court: a county employee, reporting directly to the superior court, who evaluates conservatorships and guardianships.

Joint tenancy: a method of holding property in the names of two or more people such that upon the death of one the property passes to the survivor(s).

Limited liability company: a business entity that is taxed like a partnership but affords the same protection as a corporation.

Limited partnership: a partnership in which the liability of the limited partners is restricted to their investment in the company.

Limited power of appointment: the power to direct to whom assets will ultimately pass within a limited class of beneficiaries.

Living trust: a trust established primarily for the purpose of avoiding probate that is also used as a substitute for a conservatorship.

Marital deduction, unlimited: a deduction for federal gift and estate tax purposes that allows you to make unlimited gifts to your spouse tax-free.

Marketability discount: a discount in value attributable to an asset's being subject to a buyout agreement.

Martindale-Hubbell Law Directory: a periodical that provides information on attorneys.

Medicaid: a state and federal program providing nursing home benefits.

Medicare: a federal program, run as a part of the Social Security system, providing medical benefits.

Minority discount: a discount in value attributable to an asset's not being a controlling interest.

Minor's trust: a trust, established for the benefit of a child, that terminates when the child reaches age 21.

Nomination of conservator: a document in which you nominate your conservator and, if you choose, waive any bond requirement.

Offshore trust: a trust established in a foreign country for the purpose of avoiding creditors' claims.

Pickup tax: the portion of your federal estate tax that is payable to the state in which you reside.

Pour-over will: a will that distributes your estate to your living trust.

Principal, trust: the body of a trust that usually bears interest.

Probate: the legal process for the orderly distribution of your estate.

Probate fee: the fee, established by law, to which your estate representative and the probate attorney are entitled.

QDOT trust (qualified domestic trust): a trust for the benefit of a non-citizen spouse that qualifies for the unlimited marital deduction.

QPRT trust (qualified personal residence trust): a trust into which the grantor transfers his or her residence, reserving an interest for a stated number of years, with the remainder passing usually to his or her children.

QTIP trust (qualified terminable interest property trust): a trust for the benefit of your spouse that qualifies for the unlimited marital deduction.

Qualified State Tuition Program: an educational fund you can establish for a family member that grows tax-free.

Roth IRA (Individual Retirement Account): a retirement account to which contributions are not deductible but from which distributions are tax-free.

Special needs trust: a trust for a disabled person, intended to supplement rather than replace public benefit payments.

Spendthrift provision: a trust provision that protects a beneficiary's interest in a trust from creditors' claims.

Sprinkling power: the power of a trustee to make discretionary distributions to a class of beneficiaries you designate.

Statute of Elizabeth: the first statute declaring transfers in fraud of creditors to be void.

Taxable estate: your gross estate less deductions such as debts and administration expenses.

Uniform Transfers to Minors Act: legislation providing a simple, inexpensive way to transfer property to a custodian for the benefit of a minor.

Ward: a minor for whom a guardianship has been established.

Will: a document stating how your property will be disposed of upon your death.

INDEX